ENDORSEMENTS

Misunderstandings abound when it comes to the topic of the Holy Spirit. And the implications of those misunderstandings can be spiritually catastrophic. We need the kind of help that Keith Crosby provides in this concise book, which untangles the biblical data and forthrightly drives us to think about who the Holy Spirit is, what he is dispatched to do in our world, and the relevance he should have in the heart of every follower of Christ. I trust you will appreciate the pastoral challenges at the end of each chapter and be quick to recommend this important work to others.

> — Dr. Mike Fabarez
> Senior Pastor, Compass Bible Church,
> Aliso Viejo, CA

When it comes to the Holy Spirit, some Christians are so scared of getting out on a limb that they never get up the tree. In this helpful book on the person and work of the Holy Spirit, Keith Crosby keeps it biblical, basic, and balanced. Here you will be taught that the Holy Spirit is a person to know, God come near, the author of the Bible, a cheerleader in Christian discipleship, and One who equips us and empowers us for life and godliness. This is an important book because the Holy Spirit is central to all things Christian. Use this material to get up the tree.

> — Philip De Courcy
> Senior Pastor, Kindred Community Church,
> and Teacher on Know the Word radio program,
> Anaheim Hills, CA

If you're looking for a clear introduction to the Holy Spirit, this may be the volume for you. Writing as a pastor, Keith Crosby speaks with as much clarity as charity, deftly avoiding controversy as he navigates the biblical instruction regarding the Holy Spirit. The book is a clear, insightful introduction to the third person of the Trinity, offering us tremendous aid in our earthly pilgrimage.

— Dr. Greg Cochran
 Director of Applied Theology,
 California Baptist University, Riverside, CA

Keith Crosby has done what I thought was impossible. He has provided a short *and* wide-ranging treatment of pneumatology—the doctrine of the Holy Spirit. The Third Person of the Trinity has been both misunderstood and disregarded in the minds of too many believers. This volume succinctly clarifies the confusion about the Spirit of God and practically guides the reader to worship and interact with Him. If you want to begin a more thorough understanding and relationship with the Holy Spirit, start here.

— Dr. Rick Holland
 Senior Pastor, Mission Road Bible Church,
 Kansas City, MO

While the subject of the Holy Spirit could fill volumes, Crosby's book is simple yet profound. It can help laymen, teachers and even pastors to have a clear understanding of the Holy Spirit. I found it to be a quick read, but theologically sound. I would recommend it to anyone wishing to enhance their knowledge of the Holy Spirit and His work.

— Dr. Montia Setzler
 Senior Pastor, Magnolia Church,
 Riverside, CA

Pastor Keith Crosby has written a thought-provoking book on a subject that is often seen as too mysterious, too confusing, or too controversial—so we ignore it. I appreciated Keith's clear exegesis and conversational tone, which made this analysis of the Holy Spirit's work theologically rich and easy to understand. His discussion questions and encouragement towards application will make it practical and beneficial for many.

— Amy Medina
Writer at *A Life Overseas*,
Missions Mobilizer for Reach Global,
Redlands, CA

The Word tells us all scripture is given by inspiration of God for doctrine, reproof, and instruction in righteousness. But often we read into scripture what we *wish* it said, rather than what it *actually* says. In this book, author and theologian Keith Crosby offers you this refreshing and biblically accurate depiction of the Holy Spirit that is as encouraging as it is enlightening and ultimately empowering for you, the reader.

— Craig Roberts
Bay Area Radio Host on Salem Media's KFAX-AM
1100, San Francisco, CA

The ministry of the Holy Spirit plays a very important role in the life of the believer. This is why this little book is especially valuable. Its clear and precise style, combined with a well-grounded biblical approach, helps the reader to get a sufficient understanding of the Holy Spirit and to experience the blessings of life with Him. Keith Crosby does an excellent job analyzing key passages of the Bible about the Holy Spirit and structuring them in a way that covers all major areas of the Holy Spirit's ministry.

— Aleksey Kolomiytsev
Senior Pastor, Word of Grace Bible Church,
Battle Ground, WA

This is a clear, concise, easy-to-read overview of what the Bible teaches about the Person and work of the Holy Spirit. I wholeheartedly recommend it to every believer. I really appreciate the heavy use of Scripture, rather than experiences, to help us understand God's truth about the Holy Spirit.

> — Jay Pankratz
> Senior Pastor (Emeritus), Sunrise Church,
> Rialto, CA

Extraordinary!... A book for beginners and pastors to read on the work of the Holy Spirit in salvation. A great discussion of the gospel, insight into illumination vs. revelation, practical applications, spiritual gifts held in reasonable perspective, and everything done from a clear biblical exposition.

> — James T. Darnell, Jr.
> Pastor, Author, Teacher,
> San Diego, CA

THE HOLY SPIRIT ACCORDING TO JESUS

A BEGINNER'S GUIDE TO THE THIRD PERSON OF THE TRINITY

THE HOLY SPIRIT ACCORDING TO JESUS

A BEGINNER'S GUIDE TO THE THIRD PERSON OF THE TRINITY

KEITH CROSBY

KRESS BIBLICAL RESOURCES

Published by Kress Biblical Resources
www.kressbiblical.com

ISBN: 978-1-934952-84-9

Cover Design: Reagan Schiewe
Text Design: Amy Cole, JPL Design Solutions

ACKNOWLEDGMENTS

I want to thank my family, particularly my daughters Grace Utomo and Anna Stewart, for their encouragement. It is truly a blessing to be a father of daughters. My wife, Terilyn, has been a constant presence and support in my ministry, starting with the decision to leave a comfortable life in the resort business and enter seminary at 39 years of age. Teri challenged me to make this book better. Thank you, Terilyn, for your patience and support.

I want to express my thanks to the pastors and elders of Hillside Church for allowing me a sabbatical during which I finalized and refined drafts of this book. Thank you, A.J. Hart, Gary Johnson, Mark Stickler, Jono Burlini, Jesse Fenn, Mathew Matthai, Brian Folden, John Plaza, Chuk Onwubuya, Roberto Munguìa, and Jeremy Martinez. Your patience and support over the years have been astounding.

Thanks to Rosemary Nixon, who edited a final draft of this book with great kindness and diligence, making its publication possible. Thanks also to Steve Cooley for his deep dive in the editing process, both grammatically and theologically.

Many thanks to Rick Kress of Kress Biblical Resources for taking a chance on this book. Thank you, Rick, for your encouragement, patience, and belief in this work.

Thanks to the people of Hillside Church for their numerous kindnesses to me over the last eight years of ministry. You supported me through countless hardships and loved me despite my many faults and shortcomings. Thanks, also, to the people of Sunrise Church of Rialto, who supported this work in its earlier phases when I first taught a longer version of this work as a 16-week class.

Thanks to Jay Pankratz, Senior Pastor emeritus of Sunrise Church, whose influence on my ministry cannot be overstated. You taught me to make things more accessible, simple, and clear in all aspects of ministry. I would not be here today were it not for you. The same thanks goes to Sam Forrester of Whiteside Presbyterian Church, who encouraged and mentored me long ago. Your example is one of the reasons I am in ministry and have persevered.

A word of thanks for Dr. Trevor Craigen and Dr. Larry Pettigrew, my systematic theology professors at The Master's Seminary. These men are in heaven, having received their reward for lifetimes of faithful ministry. This work would not have been possible without them.

Thanks to many unnamed friends who encouraged me through my years of ministry.

CONTENTS

INTRODUCTION: WHERE TO BEGIN?

*Those who worship him must worship him
in spirit and in truth. (John 4:24)*

The Holy Spirit can be a controversial topic of conversation in today's churches. A discussion of the Holy Spirit will probably stir up strong opinions and reactions among God's people. Part of the problem is that human beings are creatures of extremes. On the one extreme, it seems there is some fear of mentioning the Holy Spirit for fear of being labeled "one of those people" or "charismatic." Such a reluctance often leads to silence on the topic of the Holy Spirit, resulting in a misunderstanding of the things of God. On the other end of the spectrum, some seem obsessed with the Holy Spirit. It is as if the Holy Spirit has replaced the Trinity, standing head and shoulders above God the Father and God the Son. Such a view has its own devastating hazards and harms.

Thus, we come to the purpose of this book: clarity. Together, we will take this journey of discovery, reading what the Bible says about the Holy Spirit. As we consider each passage, we will look at a text and ask a series of simple questions: "What do these words say?" "What do these words mean?" "How shall we respond?" We will take a natural, commonsense reading of each text to get a true understanding of the Holy Spirit and his place in our lives. The book is divided into three sections:

"The Holy Spirit's Primary Mission," "Other Aspects of the Holy Spirit's Ministry," and "Controversies."

Let's begin!

PART ONE

THE HOLY SPIRIT'S PRIMARY MISSION

1

THE HOLY SPIRIT
ACCORDING TO JESUS

You have heard that it was said…
But I say to you…. (Matthew 5:21–22)

THE BIG QUESTION

What is the primary ministry and mission of the Holy Spirit? Many good people disagree on this matter. Is there an ultimate authority who can lead us and show us the path to the answer? Let's begin our journey with Jesus' teachings in John's Gospel. Why do we do this? In John's Gospel, Jesus offers the most extensive teaching on the Holy Spirit found anywhere in the Bible. The Apostle Paul comes second in 1 Corinthians 12–14 (we'll also look there). We do this because without Jesus, we would not have the Holy Spirit. Were it not for Jesus, we could not be "Spirit-filled." Remember that Jesus alerted his disciples to the coming of the Holy Spirit.

> These things I have spoken to you while I am still with you. But the Helper, the Holy Spirit, whom the Father will send in my name, he will teach you all things and bring to your remembrance all that I have said to you. (John 14:25–26)

What Jesus Says.

In John 14, Jesus engages in the first extensive teaching on the Holy Spirit in the New Testament, if not the entire Bible. Therefore, let's begin our study by attempting to ask and answer the question, "Just what did Jesus say about the Holy Spirit in John's Gospel?" For starters, notice what he says in John 14:16–17, 26:

> And I will ask the Father, and he will give you another Helper, to be with you forever, even the Spirit of truth, whom the world cannot receive, because it neither sees him nor knows him. You know him, for he dwells with you and will be in you…. But the Helper, the Holy Spirit, whom the Father will send in my name, he will teach you all things and bring to your remembrance all that I have said to you.

Understanding the Context.

What's Jesus saying, and why should it matter? The timing of his words carries immense weight, emphasizing the importance of this teaching as Jesus addresses his disciples on the eve of his crucifixion. He has just washed their feet as an example of the love and service of one disciple to another. The disciples must apply and model this example in the years to come (cf. John 13). What he is telling them is not trivial. Speaking just hours before his arrest and crucifixion, he tells them he is about to leave them, and they are distraught. In John 14:1–6, we find the well-known "Let not your hearts be troubled" discussion, ending in "I am the way, and the truth, and the life…." Jesus, after comforting his disciples, tells them they will not be alone nor lack resources after he leaves. He discusses the plans for their ongoing provision in ministry without him. In so doing, Jesus reveals a great deal about the Holy Spirit.

THE BIG REVEAL

Jesus reveals the primary mission or purpose of the Holy Spirit, beginning in John 14:16. He says that the Holy Spirit's role is primarily that of a "helper": "And I will ask the Father, and he will give you another Helper, to be with you forever" (John 14:16). What kind of help? The Holy Spirit, as Helper, will bring to mind all that Jesus has said, having taught them all things: "But the Helper, the Holy Spirit, whom the Father will send in my name, he will teach you all things and bring to your remembrance all that I have said to you" (John 14:26). Jesus explains that the Holy Spirit will equip believers and enable them to remember and apply the teachings of Christ to their lives and the lives of others. The Holy Spirit comes from the Father, in the name of Jesus, to do what? Jesus teaches that the primary mission of the Holy Spirit is to equip, teach, and recall to our minds Jesus' teachings. In Matthew's Gospel, we see a parallel discussion and elaboration of this mission.

> When they deliver you over, do not be anxious how you are to speak or what you are to say, for what you are to say will be given to you in that hour. *For it is not you who speak, but the Spirit of your Father speaking through you.* (Matthew 10:19–20)

Bringing Light.
Call this illumination (bringing things to light). "But the Helper, the Holy Spirit, whom the Father will send in My name, he will teach you all things and bring to your remembrance all that I have said to you" (John 14:26). Illumination differs from revelation. Revelation is revealing a new or previously unknown truth. Illumination involves the Holy Spirit, as Helper, enabling them to recall and explain what Jesus taught (i.e., what Jesus already revealed). He's bringing these things to mind and allowing them to select just the right words because God is speaking through them. We see this emphasized in another parallel passage in Luke 12:10–12:

And everyone who speaks a word against the Son of Man
will be forgiven, but the one who blasphemes against the
Holy Spirit will not be forgiven. And when they bring you
before the synagogues and the rulers and the authorities,
do not be anxious about how you should defend yourself or
what you should say, *for the Holy Spirit will teach you in that
very hour what you ought to say.*

Today, in a very real and similar sense, the Holy Spirit brings to mind all
we have learned through the Scriptures. We look to the Scriptures because,
unlike the original disciples, we are not sitting at Jesus' feet day in and day
out. Therefore, we do well not to neglect the Scriptures. Not reading something hinders the Holy Spirit bringing it to mind. With the disciples, the
Holy Spirit would bring to mind all they learned directly from Jesus during his earthly public ministry. Today, we have the completed revelation
of God in the sixty-six books of the Bible. At that time, his disciples relied
upon his teaching and explanation of the Old Testament. Today, we possess the revelation made "fully confirmed" (2 Peter 1:19). Therefore, the
Spirit brings to mind what we acquired through studying God's word. He
is as much our Helper today as he was their Helper then.

More Light, More Help.

Jesus expands upon the Holy Spirit's role as Helper in John 16. He tells
his disciples that the Helper brings Jesus' teachings to mind, working on
the hearts of believers and unbelievers, with whom the disciples speak:

And when he comes, *he will convict the world concerning sin
and righteousness and judgment:* concerning sin, because they
do not believe in me; concerning righteousness, because I
go to the Father, and you will see me no longer; concerning
judgment, because the ruler of this world is judged. I still
have many things to say to you, but you cannot bear them

now. When the Spirit of truth comes, he will guide you into all the truth, *for he will not speak on his own authority,* but whatever he hears he will speak, and he will declare to you the things that are to come. *He will glorify me, for he will take what is mine and declare it to you.* (John 16:8–14)

Here, Jesus rounds out what he taught in John 14. The Helper empowers the disciples by bringing Jesus' teachings to mind so they may recall and apply them—and teach them to others. He gives them just what they need to say, resulting in them speaking for God (God speaking through them) like prophets of old. At the same time, he does more.

More Light, More Heat.

The Spirit helps Jesus' disciples by working through them to convict the world of sin, using the disciples' words to cause the consciences of sinners to sting. In this way, even today, the Holy Spirit can use us to bring a sinner to repentance and salvation by convicting them of sinfulness, righteousness, and judgment.

Everyone possesses a conscience. Think about it. Before children do something wrong, they characteristically know to look over their shoulders in an effort to avoid detection. They seem to have some innate moral awareness. God has placed it in their hearts. They know what they are doing is wrong and check to see if "the coast is clear" because they do not wish to be caught. This is one reason that many who deny Christ often become angry when they hear the Gospel. They know that the God of the Bible exists and that they are, in some sense, accountable to him. The Holy Spirit brings this conviction to mind as part of his common grace.[1]

---

1   Common grace is the kindness that God shows to all people regardless of their relationship to him, saved or unsaved.

The French mathematician and philosopher Blaise Pascal observed that there is a void inside all people in the shape of God. Only God can fill that void by providing their conscience peace and contentment through salvation. God has put eternity in the hearts of all people. All people possess an innate sense of God's existence. He makes himself known to them through the conviction of sin. This sense of conviction exemplifies the Holy Spirit working on the conscience, convicting the world "concerning sin." This action is a genuine part of the primary mission and ministry of the Holy Spirit.

More Light, More Hope.

The Holy Spirit convicts the world of righteousness. Returning to John 16:8, "he will convict the world concerning sin and righteousness." Someone who knows what they are doing is wrong also knows what is not wrong. By implication, they see the difference between right and wrong. The Holy Spirit reinforces the message when a Christ-follower points the sinner toward the truth. In Isaiah 55:11, the prophet tells us that God's Word goes out and does not return void. God's Word accomplishes the purpose for which he sends it forth. God's Word goes out for two reasons. First, God's word goes out for salvation (or sanctification). Second, God's Word goes out for condemnation (or judgment). Upon hearing it, people understand they ignore it at their harm and peril. The Holy Spirit uses the preaching of God's word through us to point people to righteousness and to assure them or reassure us of what is right.

More Light, More Sight.

The Holy Spirit convicts the world concerning judgment. He helps sinners see things as they are. Don't miss this. "And when he comes, he will convict the world concerning sin and righteousness and judgment" (John 16:8). Convicting (convincing) people concerning sin and righteousness also points to sanctification as much as it does salvation. Convicting the world concerning judgment speaks to the fact, as Romans 1:18–24 tells us, that all people are without excuse. Jesus expands the idea: "concerning sin, because they do not believe in me; concerning righteousness, because I go to the Father, and you will see me no longer; concerning judgment, because the ruler of this world is judged" (John16:9–11). All this seems to show that when God's people share God's Word with others, the Holy Spirit helps God's people accomplish God's mission. The sharing of God's Word by God's people saves, sanctifies, convicts, or condemns people.

DIVINE GUIDANCE

What else does the Helper, the Holy Spirit, do? The Holy Spirit is the Guide who keeps the disciples of Jesus on track. The Holy Spirit seeks to move Jesus' disciples to bring glory to Christ rather than becoming distractions. How does The Holy Spirit do this?

> When the Spirit of truth comes, *he will guide you into all the truth, for he will not speak on his own authority,* but whatever he hears he will speak, and he will declare to you the things that are to come. *He will glorify me,* for he will take what is mine and declare it to you. (John 16:13–14)

There is a subtle truth here that is not to be missed. The Holy Spirit glorifies Christ, some might say, at the expense of the Spirit's own glory. We will discuss and develop this idea more fully in future paragraphs. For now, let's understand that the Holy Spirit does not call attention to Himself. Instead, he makes much of Jesus Christ.

Divine Guide.
This is one of the reasons Jesus calls the Holy Spirit "the Helper." The Holy Spirit does not lead people astray by giving them misinformation or "garbling the transmission." He cannot. He is God. As God, he is

perfect in all he does and in his communication. The Holy Spirit directs and guides Jesus' disciples, helping them find all truth. He teaches and clarifies what the disciples already know and learn so that they can be useful in ministry. He does this without calling attention to himself. His concern is not calling attention to himself but bringing glory to the Father and Son.

Divine Coach.
See the Holy Spirit like the coach "on the sidelines." Unlike "the star quarterback" (Jesus Christ), the Holy Spirit quietly provides instruction and guidance to the team from the sidelines. He is not the center of attention. He won't allow that. Sadly, John 16:13–14 troubles many who have an unbalanced view of the Holy Spirit. Why is this? First, they tend to make the Holy Spirit more prominent than the Father and Son. They overemphasize one member of the Trinity at the expense of the others, in the process misrepresenting the Holy Spirit's ministry. Second, their "prophets" give prophecies that do not come true and assign blame for this failure to the Holy Spirit. Some say the Holy Spirit cannot bring something about because others lack sufficient faith. Third, they say that while the Spirit's prophecies or messages are clear, sinful men thwart him by "garbling the transmission" like squelch and interference on an old CB radio or walkie-talkie. But the Holy Spirit is God, and his prophecies cannot fail. He won't let them.

Let's not forget that he is all-powerful, and his plans (and communication) cannot be thwarted (Isaiah 14:27; Job 42:2). Because of his omnipotence, the Holy Spirit can guide Jesus' disciples into all truth rather than into all confusion. How does this relate to him being a coach on the sidelines? He emphasizes the message, not himself. He "gets the play onto the field." What else might this involve?

Team Player.

The Holy Spirit does not call attention to himself but calls attention to Jesus. Therefore, the over-emphasis on the Holy Spirit (at the expense of Jesus) is both erroneous and unfortunate. Remember what the Scriptures say. The Holy Spirit is on a mission from the Father at the behest of the Son, "And I will ask the Father, and he will give you another Helper" (John 14:16). Jesus builds on this idea, clarifying it further in John 16:13–15:

> When the Spirit of truth comes, he will guide you into all the truth, *for he will not speak on his own authority,* but whatever he hears he will speak, and he will declare to you the things that are to come. *He will glorify me, for he will take what is mine and declare it to you.* All that the Father has is mine; *therefore I said that he will take what is mine and declare it to you.*

Just as the Son submits to the Father, the Holy Spirit submits to the Father and Son, having been sent by the Father in the Son's name (John 14:16). This ordering of titles should not be mistaken for some form of inferiority to the other members of the Trinity. The Father, the Son, and the Holy Spirit are equally and fully God but play different roles. Everyone is baptized in the name of the Father, the name of the Son, and the name of the Holy Spirit. Each member of the Trinity is equally God. Yet, each plays a different role in redemption and redemptive history. There is submission and "functional subordination" within the Trinity. Jesus clarifies this idea in John 16:13–15 (above) and the baptismal formula in the "Great Commission." The order in which they appear in the baptismal formula of the Great Commission indicates this submission.

Go therefore and make disciples of all nations, *baptizing them in the name of the Father and of the Son and of the name of the Holy Spirit*, teaching them to observe all that I have commanded you. And behold, I am with you always, to the end of the age. (Matthew 28:19–20)

This submission is not about inferiority but roles and goals within the Trinity.

EQUAL BUT...

The Holy Spirit is equally God but plays a less visible yet equally vital role as the Helper. Jesus came to glorify the Father as God in the flesh. He was God made visible to men. The Holy Spirit is invisible. The Holy Spirit's purpose is not to promote himself but to glorify the other two members of the Trinity. In John 16:13–15, Jesus informs us that the Holy Spirit says nothing on his own authority. He only speaks what he's told to speak (*"what he hears"*). He glorifies Christ and declares Jesus' teaching.

Maybe some of our discussion surprises you? It shouldn't. Read the text for yourself. Ask yourself, what do the words say? When you read these words in the Scriptures, what are they saying? What do they mean? Please don't read into the verses or passages what you wish they said. Instead, read from the verses God's message to his people, including you and me.

Avoiding Extremes, Finding Balance.
We must avoid extremes as we seek a balanced view of the Holy Spirit. Some overemphasize the Spirit at the expense of the Father and Son. They emphasize lesser aspects of the Spirit's mission and ministry at the expense of his primary mission and ministry.

We do well to follow Scriptures' teaching and the Spirit's example. While the Spirit's role is important, his role should not take center stage to the point that our view of Christ is in any way obscured. Following the Holy Spirit's example and purposes, we must make much of Jesus Christ to the glory of God the Father.

APPLICATION

Now what?

What do we do with all this information? If it only resides in our heads, it becomes little more than head knowledge. However, if it travels to our heart and takes root, this information should encourage us and move us to action. Consider the following responses to what Jesus says about the Holy Spirit.

Rejoice!

Jesus and his Father sent us a helper like Jesus, who is with us and will live within us forever! We are not alone, powerless, or without resources. Jesus did not leave us as orphans. Rejoice, taking stock in the fact that we can live Spirit-empowered, supernatural lives.

Read.

Sometimes, people use reading plans to read through the Bible in a year. That's great and profitable. But we are called to investigate God's Word so that we can be "approved workman unashamed" (2 Timothy 2:15). As you read, pray: "Open my eyes that I may see wonderful things in your law" (Psalm 119:18). Let the Holy Spirit bring to light what is written in the Scriptures so that he may bring it to mind when you need it.

Memorize.

The Psalmist says, "I have stored up your word in my heart, that I might not sin against you" (Psalm 119:11). The Holy Spirit will bring those texts you memorize to mind under the most challenging and unusual circumstances. He will bring them to mind and use them to guide you into all truth. He will also use this memorized Word to speak through you as a follower of Jesus Christ. He will provide you with what you need to say at the appropriate time—if you take the time to memorize Scripture.

Ask.

Jesus has not left you and me without resources. He has transmitted and preserved the Scriptures for our study that we might find guidance and encouragement (Romans 15:4). Prayerfully ask the Holy Spirit's guidance as you read, study, and memorize his Scriptures so that you can make much of Christ: "He will glorify me, for he will take what is mine and declare it to you. All that the Father has is mine; therefore I said that he will take what is mine and declare it to you" (John 16:14–15).

Trust.

Know that in the Holy Spirit you have a Helper like Jesus. The Father and the Son have given us a Helper who, like Jesus, is God. Depend upon him. Trust him: "Trust in the LORD with all your heart, and do not lean on your own understanding. In all your ways acknowledge him, and he will make straight your paths" (Proverbs 3:5–6).

FOR FURTHER THOUGHT

1. Based upon the teachings of the Lord Jesus Christ in John 14 and 16, what is the primary mission and ministry of the Holy Spirit?

2. How does Jesus' description of the primary mission and ministry of the Holy Spirit compare with your prior understanding? Are they similar, different, or very different? What should you do to move closer to his position? What adjustments will you make?

3. If you strongly disagree with what we've discussed, will you commit to re-reading John 13–16 like a good Berean to see if these things are true?

4. How does John 16:13–14 appear to refute or contradict the teachings and practices of those who overemphasize the Holy Spirit at the expense of the Father and Son? How does this relate to the picture of the Holy Spirit as a coach on the sidelines?

PART TWO

OTHER ASPECTS OF THE SPIRIT'S MINISTRY

2

THE NATURE OF
THE HOLY SPIRIT
(HE, SHE, OR IT?)

You are witnesses of these things. And behold,
I am sending the promise of my Father upon you.
But stay in the city until you are clothed with power
from on high. (Luke 24:48–49)

We've discussed the mission and ministry of the Holy Spirit, but who is he? The cultist would ask, "What is it?" A Jehovah's Witness will insist that the Holy Spirit is a force—a thing. It's as if the Holy Spirit is a rock, a stone, or something like radiation, a force: an "it." Popular books and novels have depicted the Holy Spirit as an Asian woman! Others appeal to intuition. Let's look to God's word for answers to this question.

CLARITY IS OUR AIM

Our aim is to be clear on who and what the Holy Spirit is. We want to understand "what" the Holy Spirit is regarding nature, character, gender, and behavior. We must always ask, "What does the Bible say?" After all, it is through the Bible that we learn what Jesus teaches. Through the Bible, we understand what the Holy Spirit says about himself.

Not an "It!"

Let's be clear. The Bible teaches us that the Holy Spirit is not an "it." We see this very clearly and unmistakably in Acts 13:1–4. Here, the Holy Spirit, himself makes this abundantly clear.

> Now there were in the church at Antioch prophets and teachers, Barnabas, Simeon who was called Niger, Lucius of Cyrene, Manaen a member of the court of Herod the tetrarch, and Saul. While they were worshiping the Lord and fasting, *the Holy Spirit said, "Set apart for me Barnabas and Saul for the work to which I have called them."* Then after fasting and praying they laid their hands on them and sent them off. So, being sent out by the Holy Spirit, they went down to Seleucia, and from there they sailed to Cyprus. (Acts 13:1–4)

He Speaks.

What do we learn from this passage? The Holy Spirit is not an "it," like a rock or a force, because he expresses himself through intelligible speech and ideas. "While they were worshiping the Lord and fasting, the Holy Spirit said…" (Acts 13:2). Consider the implications of verse 2. Rocks do not speak; radiation does not speak. Intelligent beings speak. The Holy Spirit speaks.

Personality?

The Holy Spirit displays aspects of personality. He exhibits intellectual faculties and self-awareness. A self-aware being expresses his will, commands, or desires: "Set apart for me Barnabas and Saul for the work to which I have called them" (Acts 13:2). We see that the Holy Spirit is self-aware. He speaks using personal pronouns like "me," "my," and "I."

He Thinks.

The Holy Spirit exercises his will and expresses his desires as an intelligent being. The Holy Spirit verbalizes and communicates his desire and will: "Set apart for me...." Again, rocks, trees, radiation, and wind have neither a will nor a means to articulate desire (or a course of action). The Holy Spirit does. These are aspects of personality. In Acts 13:4, we see that the Holy Spirit sent out Barnabas and Saul (later called Paul) on a mission he had for them: "So, being sent out by the Holy Spirit, they went down to Seleucia, and from there they sailed to Cyprus" (Acts 13:4). The Holy Spirit exercises will (and authority). He gives commands. These are all aspects of personality.

Feelings.

Beyond will and intellect, the Holy Spirit manifests the faculty of emotion. The Bible shows us that the Holy Spirit has feelings: "And do not grieve the Holy Spirit of God, by whom you were sealed for the day of redemption" (Ephesians 4:30). Can we make a rock or the wind feel sad? Do "things" have feelings or grieve? The Bible shows us that God displays a full range of emotions: anger (Romans 1:18; Zephaniah 3:8), compassion (Psalm 145:8–9), joy (2 Samuel 22:20; Nehemiah 8:10), love (John 3:16; 1 John 4:8). God has emotions; therefore, the Holy Spirit has emotions.

Satisfaction.

Within the realm of emotions or feelings, the Holy Spirit experiences satisfaction. When the Apostles in Jerusalem sent a delegation to the non-Jewish churches to settle matters about Gentiles and Law-keeping, they wrote: "For it has seemed good to the Holy Spirit and to us to lay on you no greater burden than these requirements:" (Acts 15:28). What's going on here? Like us, created in his image and likeness, the Holy Spirit experiences satisfaction. It is fair to say that the Holy Spirit has emotions, sensibilities, preferences, and intellect. We say he is like us, but of course, we are like him since God created human beings in his image and like-ness. We are like him in that we bear his image and likeness in terms of faculties of personality. So what? The wind does not have emotions. The rocks do not have emotions. "Things" do not have emotions. Beings with personality have emotions. The Holy Spirit is not an "it" but a "he." He has emotions and feelings.

A "He!"

Why insist the Holy Spirit is a "he?" Can we? We can. Where does he describe himself as "he?" Not to get too technical, but New Testament Greek has three gender descriptions: feminine, masculine, and neuter. The gender used for the Holy Spirit is male. But you don't have to be a Greek scholar to see this. His gender becomes quite apparent. Your English language Bible makes this plain enough. This gender distinc-tion is not an act of chauvinism but a revelation from God. Returning to our previous discussion of the Holy Spirit's mission based on John 14 and John 16, we read this: "But the Helper, the Holy Spirit, whom the Father will send in my name, *he* will teach you all things and bring to your remembrance all that I have said to you" (John 14:26). The Lord Jesus repeatedly refers to the Holy Spirit as a "he." Jesus does this not once but often. Count the "he's," the "his's," and the "him" (i.e., personal pronouns) in the following passage:

> Nevertheless, I tell you the truth: it is to your advantage that I go away, for if I do not go away, the Helper will not come to you. But if I go, I will send *him* to you. And when *he* comes, *he* will convict the world concerning sin and righteousness and judgment: concerning sin, because they do not believe in me; concerning righteousness, because I go to the Father, and you will see me no longer; concerning judgment, because the ruler of this world is judged. "I still have many things to say to you, but you cannot bear them now. When

the Spirit of truth comes, *he* will guide you into all the truth, for *he* will not speak on *his* own authority, but whatever *he* hears *he* will speak, and *he* will declare to you the things that are to come. *He* will glorify me, for *he* will take what is mine and declare it to you. (John 16:7–14)

Neither She Nor It.

As discussed, the Holy Spirit is a "he," not an "it" (or a "her"). He is not a "thing" like a rock or a "force" like the wind. Rocks don't have genders, the wind is neither male nor female, and forces don't have genders. However, individual beings have genders. The Holy Spirit (like God the Father and the Son) is a "he." This is how the Lord Jesus Christ describes him. Follow Jesus' example.

WORSHIP IS YOUR AIM

By now, it should be clear that the Holy Spirit is God. Earlier, we alluded to and discussed the Holy Spirit being of the exact nature and essence as Jesus and the Father. Jesus promised to send another helper to replace him because Jesus was going to the Father: "And I will ask the Father, and he will give you another helper, to be with you forever, even the Spirit of truth" (John 14:16–17). The specific wording in the original Greek speaks to another helper of the same kind. He repeats this promise of "another helper" in John 14:28. Lacking an understanding of biblical Greek, you cannot discern this from the context. But Jesus is implying a sameness or similarity. This sameness in nature and essence speaks to the Godhood, or deity, of the Holy Spirit.

Does John 14:16–17 imply Deity or Godhood? Can we say that the Holy Spirit is God based on this passage? Jesus is God (John 1:1–3, 14). Therefore, the Holy Spirit is God—another helper like Jesus—of the same kind.

Blasphemy.

When one slanders God, it is considered blasphemy. Blasphemy is an act of disrespect or sacrilege against a god or God. Touching on the cultist's understanding of the Holy Spirit, the Spirit as a "he" cannot be an "it." Have you ever tried to insult or offend a thing, a rock, the wind, or a force? You can't.

Forces, things, and "it's" do not possess consciousness or self-awareness, thus they cannot be offended. They are immune to insults because they lack personality. They are inanimate, unthinking, and unfeeling. You can insult beings with identity, sensitivity, and understanding. This is another reason the Holy Spirit is not an "it." The Holy Spirit as God can be blasphemed (at great peril). Jesus tells us as much in this famous and famously frightening passage:

> "Truly, I say to you, all sins will be forgiven the children of man, and whatever blasphemies they utter, *but whoever blasphemes against the Holy Spirit* never has forgiveness, but is guilty of an eternal sin"—for they were saying, "He has an unclean spirit." (Mark 3:28–30)

Among other things, to blaspheme (the act of blasphemy) means to slander someone. Can you or I insult a rock? Can we offend the wind? Can we speak against a force as if it were an individual? No, we cannot. Remember this the next time a cultist knocks on your door.

Deity.

Some still ask, "Does the Bible really indicate that the Holy Spirit is God?" Yes, it does. Perhaps the most straightforward place is in Acts 5:1–5:

> But a man named Ananias, with his wife Sapphira, sold a piece of property, and with his wife's knowledge he kept back

for himself some of the proceeds and brought only a part of it and laid it at the apostles' feet. But Peter said, "Ananias, *why has Satan filled your heart to lie to the Holy Spirit* and to keep back for yourself part of the proceeds of the land? While it remained unsold, did it not remain your own? And after it was sold, was it not at your disposal? *Why is it that you have contrived this deed in your heart? You have not lied to men but to God."* When Ananias heard these words, he fell down and breathed his last. And great fear came upon all who heard of it.

Here, the Apostle Peter, is moved by the Holy Spirit, refers to the Holy Spirit as God. He tells Ananias that lying to the Holy Spirit is lying to God. The deity of the Holy Spirit, the God-ness of the Holy Spirit, goes hand in hand with our earlier discussion of Acts 13:

Now there were in the church at Antioch prophets and teachers, Barnabas, Simeon who was called Niger, Lucius of Cyrene, Manaen a member of the court of Herod the tetrarch, and Saul. While they were worshiping the Lord and fasting, *the Holy Spirit said, "Set apart for me Barnabas and Saul for the work to which I have called them."* Then after fasting and praying they laid their hands on them and sent them off. *So, being sent out by the Holy Spirit,* they went down to Seleucia, and from there they sailed to Cyprus. (Acts 13:1–4)

Does this passage (Acts 13:1–4) come close to implying or affirming the deity of the Holy Spirit? Ask yourself, "What were the disciples doing in this passage?" They were worshipping and fasting. Also implicit in this passage is that they were praying. Who responds to their prayers, worship, and fasting? As they were fasting and praying (during a time of worship) the Holy Spirit (God) spoke to them about sending Barnabas and Saul out as missionaries. The Holy Spirit singles them out for a mission to which he has called them. It would seem clear that the Holy Spirit is God, as much as Jesus and the Father are God. Like them, he responds to prayer and worship.

Anything Else?

There are other examples of the Scriptures pointing to the deity of the Holy Spirit. Jesus Christ gave the Holy Spirit equal prominence with God the Father and himself, God the Son, as he gave instructions for baptism in Matthew 28:19. "Go therefore and make disciples of all nations, baptizing them in the name of the Father and of the Son and of the Holy Spirit," (Matthew 28:19). Notice a couple of things: Father, Son, and Holy Spirit share equality and, apparently, a common 'name' or character. Jesus did *not* say baptize "in the names of the Father, Son, and Holy Spirit." Here, Jesus gives the Holy Spirit (and himself) equal billing, or prominence, with God the Father.

The Holy Spirit was present and active at creation (like the rest of the Trinity). Colossians 1:15–16 tells us that Christ is the Creator: "He is the image of the invisible God, the firstborn of all creation. For by him all things were created, in heaven and on earth, visible and invisible, whether thrones or dominions or rulers or authorities—all things were created through him and for him." John 1:3 also reminds us that there is nothing made that Jesus didn't make. So we know that Christ, the Creator, was active in the creation, and the Spirit was there with him. Jesus created light; the Spirit hovered above the waters (Genesis 1:3–4):

> And the Spirit of God was hovering over the face of the waters. And God said, "Let there be light," and there was light. And God saw that the light was good. And God separated the light from the darkness.

The Trinity.

What about the Holy Spirit and the Trinity? In Genesis 1:3–4 and Matthew 28:19–20, we also see evidence of the Trinity. Speaking of the Trinity, there are those who, like the Jehovah's Witnesses, deny the existence of the Trinity. In the interest of space, we will not discuss this issue fully here.

Modalists?

Modalists believe that there is no Trinity and that God the Father, Son, and Holy Spirit are simply manifestations of God where God appears differently at different times. They argue that God appears at other times in various modes of expression. These groups deny that God can be "three-in-one."

Present All at Once!

Beyond the baptismal formula given by Jesus, we have the very baptism of Jesus as proof that the Father, Son, and Holy Spirit are not modes of God. Each is fully God and separately a member of the Trinity. God does not change masks in each vignette of his unfolding drama of redemption. We see this clearly at the baptism of Jesus Christ, which is contained in the passage below.

> And when Jesus was baptized, *immediately he went up from the water,* and behold, the heavens were opened to him, and *he saw the Spirit of God descending like a dove and coming to rest on him*; and behold, *a voice from heaven said, "This is my beloved Son, with whom I am well pleased."* Then *Jesus was led up by the Spirit* into the wilderness to be tempted by the devil. (Matthew 3:16–4:1)

All three members of the Trinity are present at the baptism of Jesus. They are simultaneously present. The Father speaks as the Spirit descends like a dove (vv. 3:16b–17) as the Son emerges from the waters of baptism (v. 3:16a). One can't help but notice that the Holy Spirit leads Jesus into the desert to be tempted (v. 4:1). The Trinity exists. Each member is God. God the Holy Spirit is always God and always the third member of the Trinity. God the Father is always God and always the Father, the first member of the Trinity. God the Son is always God and always the Son, the second member of the Trinity. This reality enables us to conclude several truths about the Holy Spirit, his nature, essence, and deity.

Always God.
Let's review and expand on a few ideas. It's safe to say that the Holy Spirit is not an "it" but a "he." He's not a "thing" but a person. He expresses opinions, desires, feelings, and gives commands. The Holy Spirit refers to himself ("I"). It is possible to grieve and insult him (blaspheme). The Holy Spirit is not an "it."

Without a doubt, the Holy Spirit is God. As we saw in Acts 5, lying to the Holy Spirit is lying to God. Elsewhere, Jesus describes the Holy Spirit as another helper like Jesus, having the exact divine nature, essence, and Godhood. Jesus ranks the Holy Spirit alongside himself and God the Father in the baptism command. The Holy Spirit is equally God with the Father and Jesus.

It's safe to say that the Holy Spirit is a member of the Trinity and that the Trinity exists. We see the Holy Spirit present alongside Jesus in Creation, hovering over the waters' face. The Holy Spirit, along with the Father, is present at Jesus' baptism. Since the Holy Spirit is God, how shall we respond to this truth?

APPLICATION

What do we do with all this teaching or information? Put it to work in your life and share it with others. Here are two straightforward yet incredibly impactful places to begin (they have more significance than you realize). How do we respond to what we learned?

Plan for Changes.
Determine to make small yet significant adjustments to your behavior. Remember that the Holy Spirit is God, not an "it." Adjust your speech accordingly. It is not appropriate to refer to him as an "it." Often, this is hard because we tend to refer to people by familiar names: Jim, Raul, Margarita, etc. Would you refer to Jesus as "it?" Would you refer to God the Father as "it?" Don't refer to the Holy Spirit as "it."

Engage in Self-Examination.
Reconsider your habits and practices. What do we mean by this? Later, we will study and learn about what it means to be Temples of the Holy Spirit (1 Corinthians 6:19). We've already learned that Jesus promised (and this has come to pass) that the Holy Spirit will both be with us and in us forever (John 14:17). Realize, therefore, that the Holy Spirit sees what you see, he hears what you hear, he sees what you are thinking, and goes where you go. So what? Just as you wouldn't take your grandmother to see certain movies or places or engage in certain activities, show the same reverence and respect to the Holy Spirit. He is, after all, God.

FOR FURTHER THOUGHT

1. Some describe the Holy Spirit as an "it." Others describe the Holy Spirit as "she." Jesus describes the Holy Spirit as a "he" (John 16:7–14). What do Jesus' words in this passage tell us about the Holy Spirit regarding gender?

2.   Remember our discussions about the faculties of personality. How might this pertain to Acts 13:1–4? What might this teach us about the Holy Spirit and his "self-awareness?" Why would this passage lead us to conclude that the Holy Spirit is not an "it?"

3.   Some like to think of the Holy Spirit as a force. Others point out that the Scriptures show that the Holy Spirit is God. Which view does Acts 5:1–5 seem to support? How might this relate to Matthew 28:19–20? How might these relate to Jesus' comments of his disciples receiving from the Father, at his behest, another helper like Jesus (John 14:16–19)?

4.   Reread Matthew 3:16–4:1. Why would these verses be problematic for a modalist? How do they point to the existence of the Trinity? How might they relate to the baptismal formula that Jesus later gives in Matthew 28:18–20?

5.   How has this chapter, if at all, clarified or challenged your understanding of the nature and identity of the Holy Spirit? How will you implement these changes in your practice?

3

THE HOLY SPIRIT AND INSPIRATION

Now while the Pharisees were gathered together, Jesus asked them a question, saying, "What do you think about the Christ? Whose son is he?" They said to him, "The son of David." He said to them, "How is it then that David, in the Spirit, calls him Lord, saying, "'The Lord said to my Lord, "Sit at my right hand, until I put your enemies under your feet."'"
(Matthew 22:41–44)

QUESTIONS, QUESTIONS...

Where do the Scriptures come from? How did we "get" the Scriptures? Did human beings make them up or invent them? Why do we look to the Bible as authoritative in any way? Are the Scriptures (is the Bible) useful? Did God dictate them to people over time? 2 Timothy 3 provides the answer.

All Scripture is breathed out by God and profitable for teaching, for reproof, for correction, and for training in righteousness, that the man of God may be complete, equipped for every good work. (2 Timothy 3:16–17)

Maybe you learned this verse as a new believer. It's a familiar passage to many. I memorized it when being mentored by the Navigators. Some translations read "inspired by God." Whether your Bible version reads "God-breathed," "breathed out by God," or "inspired," the idea is the same. The Source of the Scriptures is God. The Holy Spirit, Himself, breathed out the Scriptures.

Inspiration ("Breathed Out").

The Scriptures "come from within God." Some refer to this concept as the "doctrine of inspiration." The Apostle Peter explains it this way:

> No prophecy of Scripture comes from someone's own inter-
> pretation. For no prophecy was ever produced by the will of
> man, but men spoke from God as they were carried along by
> the Holy Spirit. (2 Peter 1:20–21)

God moved men to write the words of God. These writings are the words of God and, as such, the word of God, the Bible. Returning to the passage we used to open this chapter, we see Jesus himself saying the same thing and giving us a clue who the author of Scripture is. Who breathed out or inspired the word of God that we hold in our hands today? Jesus tells us in Matthew 22:41–44. Here, Jesus is speaking with the Pharisees and refers to Psalm 110:1, which David wrote by the Holy Spirit.[2]

> Now while the Pharisees were gathered together, Jesus
> asked them a question, saying, "What do you think about

---

2   The LORD says to my Lord: "Sit at my right hand, until I make your enemies your footstool (Psalm 110:1)."

the Christ? Whose son is he?" They said to him, "The son of David." He said to them, "How is it then that David, *in the Spirit*, calls him Lord, saying, "'The Lord said to my Lord, "Sit at my right hand, until I put your enemies under your feet"'"? (Matthew 22:41–44)

Don't miss that Jesus' words tell us much about how the Jewish people understood inspiration. Jesus speaks to the gathering of the Pharisees using terminology that they understood and were accustomed to using. The Pharisees (and many other Jewish leaders) may have disagreed with Jesus on many things. But they all understood the concept of the inspiration of Scripture. This is an integral part of the ministry and mission of the Holy Spirit.

Not Robots, Not Dictation.

The idea is that God, in this case, the Holy Spirit, took the writers of the Scriptures (Moses, Matthew, Mark, Isaiah, etc.) and moved them to write just what God wanted them to, but in their own words and style. This wasn't dictation. They were not robots. They were unique human beings. The Holy Spirit moved them and allowed them to retain their individuality while writing in a way that those around them would understand.

Plenary What?

Theologians and Bible scholars call this "plenary verbal inspiration." That means what we read is only what God intended and moved these men to write. They did not write one word more or one idea less than they should have. Once again, this is not dictation but something more. It's not like Jesus (or anyone else) showed up and said to a scribe, personal secretary, or assistant, "Write this down." It's different—quite different. Every word is God's word, yet men write in their own way or style.

Their Words, God's Words.

What they wrote is the inspired Word of God. Every word and thought are God's. This is often a complex concept to grasp (like the Trinity), but we must learn and understand it. After all, our faith is rational, not irrational. Our faith is a thoughtful, reasonable faith, as opposed to a blind faith.

Not Just "Inspiring Literature."

Let's not misunderstand what we mean by "inspiration." The Holy Spirit's inspiration of the text is not the inspiration of the men. In literature, we often read inspirational reading. There is prose or literature that *inspires* us. This is not the same as the biblical concept. The Holy Spirit moved and carried along the men who wrote Scripture to write God's inspired Word. This inspiration leads to a revelation and understanding made more sure. Now, you might ask: "Where in the Bible do we read this?" The fact is, we do in fact learn this from the Bible:

> *And we have the prophetic word more fully confirmed,* to which you will do well to pay attention as to a lamp shining in a dark place, until the day dawns and the morning star rises in your hearts, knowing this first of all, *that no prophecy of Scripture comes from someone's own interpretation.* For no prophecy was ever produced by the will of man, but men spoke from God as *they were carried along by the Holy Spirit.* (2 Peter 1:19–21)

In this passage, Peter is writing to believers about hearing God's audible voice at the transfiguration of Jesus Christ, when Jesus' normal earthly appearance was rolled back, and he shone like the sun as he spoke with Moses and Elijah. Peter says something extraordinary about the Christians receiving Peter's epistle, or letter. Notice what Peter says:

1. They, the recipients of Peter's letter, have access to a revelation from God made more sure that they should pay attention to (v. 19). The written Scripture (i.e., "prophecy of Scripture") is better than an audible prophecy.

2. This prophecy, or prophetic word made "more fully confirmed," is the teaching or prophecy of God recorded in the Scriptures (v. 20). It's written for all believers in that it's not for uniquely personal or private interpretation. There are no stock investment tips just for you. The principles apply to the whole church: "knowing this first of all, that no prophecy of Scripture comes from someone's own interpretation" (v. 20).

3. Such prophecies aren't given by the will of man (v. 21). This has a two-fold meaning. The prophecy does not originate with man. Man has no control over the timing and giving of the prophecy. God, the Holy Spirit, is in control.

4. The men who wrote the Scriptures (i.e., the prophecy of Scripture) were moved and carried along by the Holy Spirit to say and write what they wrote (v. 21). The Holy Spirit inspired the words they wrote, moving and carrying them along.

ACCEPT NO SUBSTITUTES

Your Bible is the revelation made more sure than any other revelation you can receive. What's the big deal here? It's this. You have it in your hands. God ensured that all you needed for matters of faith and practice was written down. He preserved it for your use, repeated study, reflection, memorization, meditation, and encouragement that you might have hope (Romans 15:4). You don't have to rely on anyone else to understand it. It's right there in your hand. The Holy Spirit provided it. It is complete, and the Holy Spirit will use it to guide you into all truth (John 16:13). Accept no substitutes (2 Peter 1:19–21; 2 Timothy 3:16–17).

No Expiration Dates.

The Scriptures are God-breathed. This makes them reliable because, like God, they never go out of date. They remain relevant until heaven and earth pass away, from the Old Testament to the New Testament. Jesus puts it this way:

> For truly, I say to you, *until heaven and earth pass away,* not an iota, not a dot, will pass from the Law until all is accomplished. Therefore whoever relaxes one of the least of these commandments and teaches others to do the same will be called least in the kingdom of heaven, but whoever does them and teaches them will be called great in the kingdom of heaven. (Matthew 5:18–19)

As you read this, are heaven and earth still here? Heaven and earth have not passed away.

There's nothing quite like the Bible. Inspiration of the Holy Spirit means the Scriptures are like God: error-free. Inspiration by the Holy Spirit means the Scriptures are like God in that they are eternal. They cannot fail. Jesus said, "Scripture cannot be broken" (John 10:35). The Scriptures cannot steer us wrong. They are, like God, infallible and inerrant. They say what they mean. They mean what they say. They are reliable. How does this relate to the Holy Spirit? Maybe you've noticed one of my favorite catchphrases: "The Holy Spirit tells us through the pen of the Apostle Paul...." Perhaps you've noticed I've written something like "The Holy Spirit wrote through the pen of the prophet Isaiah." I say this because everything you read in your Bibles is not private prophecies or musings from men. These words are the Word of God. These words are sure, trustworthy, and perfect.

A few paragraphs back, we referred to 2 Timothy 3:16–17: "All Scripture is breathed out by God and profitable for teaching, for reproof, for correction, and for training in righteousness, that the man of God may be complete, equipped for every good work." This is a policy statement on the ramifications and impact of the Holy Spirit's inspired Scripture. What does it tell us?

1. The Bible is useful for many things: teaching us, putting us in our place, helping us adjust our lives, and showing us how to live rightly.

2. The Spirit-inspired Scriptures equip us to face every situation and circumstance in this life.

3. The Scriptures have something to say about every inch of thread that makes up the fabric of our existence.

They are the revelation made more sure. David, "in the Spirit," writes this:

> *The law of the LORD is perfect,* reviving the soul; *the testimony of the LORD is sure,* making wise the simple; *the precepts of the LORD are right,* rejoicing the heart; the commandment of the LORD is pure, enlightening the eyes; *the fear of the LORD is clean,* enduring forever; *the rules of the LORD* are true, and righteous altogether. More to be desired are they than gold, even much fine gold; sweeter also than honey and drippings of the honeycomb. Moreover, *by them* is your servant warned; *in keeping them* there is great reward. (Psalm 19:7–11)

The first half of Psalm 19 is about knowing about God through the handiwork of his creation. The second half of Psalm 19 is about understanding God (knowing him) through the pages of Scripture. These Scriptures are from the Holy Spirit. They are his inspired words.

All God-breathed.

All Scripture is God-breathed (2 Timothy 3:16). The Holy Spirit breathed out all the Scriptures. Consider that when the Spirit moved Paul to write 2 Timothy, the Bible of the Church was the Old Testament or Jewish Bible. What about the New Testament? It's all God-breathed.

Red-letter Christians?

It's fashionable today to "unhitch" from the Old Testament and disregard most of the New Testament (like the Epistles). That's over 90% of the Bible! Some say they prefer to stick with the so-called "red letters" of the Gospels (Jesus' words) than the words of others, like Paul. But the Apostles recognized the work of other apostles (and their assistants) as Scripture. The Apostle Paul recognized the writings of Luke as the Bible.

"All Scripture" means just that, "all of the Scriptures" are God-breathed (2 Timothy 3:16). No part of Scripture is less or more inspired than others. The writings of Moses in the Ten Commandments hold no less significance than the Words of Jesus recorded in Luke or Matthew's Sermon on the Mount (or John's Upper Room Discourse). The Words of Jesus in the Lord's prayer are no more inspired than the writings of Paul. The New Testament passages are just as inspired as the Old Testament. Scripture says so, putting the writing of Luke on par with the writing of Moses in 1 Timothy 5:18, "For the Scripture says, "You shall not muzzle an ox when it treads out the grain," and, "The laborer deserves his wages." The Holy Spirit has moved the Apostle Paul to refer to an Old Testament passage and New Testament passage side by side as Scripture:

- You shall not muzzle an ox when it is treading out the grain. (Deuteronomy 25:4)

- And remain in the same house, eating and drinking what they provide, for the laborer deserves his wages. Do not go from house to house. (Luke 10:7)

Notice that Paul also puts the words of Moses and the words of Jesus on the same level. The Apostles realized that they (and each other) wrote Scripture. Peter affirmed the letters of Paul were Scripture.

> And count the patience of our Lord as salvation, just as our beloved brother Paul also wrote to you according to the wisdom given him, as he does in all his letters when he speaks in them of these matters. There are some things in them that are hard to understand, which the ignorant and unstable twist to their own destruction, as they do *the other Scriptures*. (2 Peter 3:15–16)

The New American Standard Bible renders this passage more apparent and more convincing.

> and regard the patience of our Lord as salvation; just as also our beloved brother Paul, according to the wisdom given him, wrote to you, as also in all his letters, speaking in them of these things, in which are some things hard to understand, which the untaught and unstable distort, as they do also *the rest of the Scriptures*, to their own destruction. (2 Peter 3:15–16 NASB)

All Letters are "Red!"

Peter is saying that the writings of Paul are Scripture. He favorably compares them to the rest of the Scriptures. So what? What's the big deal? There is no room for you or me to tamper with this revelation made more sure that it is the word of God. Paul's writings are just as inspired by the Holy Spirit as Jesus' Words in the Gospels or the first three chapters of Genesis. We don't get to pick and choose one passage over and against another. All letters are "red."

APPLICATION

Now what? Now is the time to think about how you see, or have seen, the Scriptures. Now may be the time to rethink your approach to the Scriptures and life. Consider the implications of "God-breathed."

Trustworthy and Reliable.
Please realize that the Scriptures are trustworthy because they are God-breathed. They say what they mean, and they mean what they say in plain language. When the Scriptures say that Jonah was in the belly of the fish for three days, the Scriptures mean what they say. Realize that when we read that Joshua and his armies marched around Jericho for seven days and that and Jesus was in the tomb for three days the Scriptures mean what they say. Days mean days, not weeks, months, years, decades, centuries, or ages. The Holy Spirit communicated truth to us in terms that we can understand. That truth is reliable.

You Can't Pick and Choose.
Know that you can't selectively choose which Scriptures are inspired or not. All Scriptures are inspired by God, not just the ones we like. By following the teachings of Scripture concerning contemporary issues, you will never be on the wrong side of history. History, on the other hand, may well be on the wrong side of God (Proverbs 30:5).

Always Applicable.
Understand that regardless of what part of the Scriptures you are reading, it holds relevance to you, in the present moment, as much as it did to those then and there when it was given. There is a principle to follow,

a prohibition to observe, and a prescription for your life. The Scriptures have something to say about every inch of thread that makes up the fabric of our existence (2 Timothy 3:17).

Timeless.

Like God the Holy Spirit, the Scriptures are timeless, eternal, and unchanging (1 Peter 1:25). They have no expiration date. Trust them, embrace them, read them, study them, learn them, and apply them.

Please study them.

Ready yourself to be like a noble Berean to test every truth claim and prophecy you hear outside the Bible to see if it aligns with the Holy Spirit-inspired Word of God. Test the spirits to see if they are from God. Study to show yourself an approved workman who rightly handles the word of truth (2 Timothy 2:15).

FOR FURTHER THOUGHT

1. Read Matthew 22: 41–44. How does what Jesus says about inspiration connect with 2 Timothy 3:16? How does David, being "in the Spirit," connect with 2 Peter 1:20–21?

2. How does 2 Timothy 3:17 relate to 1 Peter 1:25 regarding the timeless truth of Scripture and the concept of the Bible becoming obsolete?

3. How does 2 Peter 1:17–21 point to the fact that the Scriptures are more reliable than any prophecy any human today might try to give you? Relate this to 2 Timothy 3:16–17 and Psalm 19:7–14.

4. Are the Old Testament and New Testament writings both Scripture? How does 1 Timothy 5:18 point to this? Learn to explain this to others.

5.   How does 2 Peter 3:15–16 point to the writings of Paul as Scripture? Write a brief explanation you can use with others with similar questions.

4

THE HOLY SPIRIT AND YOUR SALVATION

It is the Spirit who gives life;
the flesh is no help at all. (John 6:63)

SEVENTY TIMES SEVEN

Why doesn't everyone respond to the gospel the first time they hear it? Often, people cite statistics indicating the average convert hears the gospel seven times before being saved. Is that true? Sometimes it seems like "seventy times seven and not at all!" Many people understand that it's not how many times you hear the gospel that matters but how and why you respond to it. This brings us to the odd and not-so-little term: "regeneration."

What's in a Word?
What is regeneration? What does regeneration have to do with how people respond to the gospel? What does regeneration have to do with the Holy Spirit? Regeneration is part of the work of the Holy Spirit in our salvation and is part of and a result of the Holy Spirit's work in salvation.

45

Like a Dead Battery.

Think of regeneration as putting jumper cables on a dead battery. Consider regeneration as the emergency room doctor putting the defibrillating paddles on a stopped heart to bring life. One Bible scholar puts it this way:

> [Regeneration is the] inner cleansing and renewal of the human nature by the Holy Spirit. Mankind's spiritual condition is transformed from a disposition of sin to one of a new relationship with God (Ti 3:5). Regeneration involves both moral restoration and the reception of new life.... The process of regeneration is not brought about by human righteousness but by the gracious act of God (Eph 2:8,9).[3]

Why do we need regeneration? Before salvation, before the intervention of the Holy Spirit, you and I were spiritually dead. We could not understand, let alone respond to spiritual truth (1 Corinthians 2:14). You could say that we were dead to God. From our dead vantage point God was dead to us. We were (are) unable and unwilling to desire a right relationship with God:

> And *you were dead in the trespasses and sins* in which you once walked, following the course of this world, following the prince of the power of the air, the spirit that is now at work in the sons of disobedience—among whom we all once lived in the passions of our flesh, carrying out the desires of the body and the mind, and were by nature children of wrath, like the rest of mankind. But God, being rich in mercy, because of the great love with which he loved us, even when we were

---

3   "Regeneration," *Baker Encyclopedia of the Bible*, ed. Walter A. Elwell (Grand Rapids: Baker Book House, 1988), 2:1830.

dead in our trespasses, *made us alive together with Christ*—by grace you have been saved—(Ephesians 2:1–5).

The Holy Spirit, speaking through the pen of Paul, explains that God had to make us alive in Christ to save us. This is regeneration. Why is this? Our minds and our hearts were broken and dead. But couldn't we some-how figure out our need for the Savior and respond? The Holy Spirit answers this question for us:

> *The natural person does not accept the things of the Spirit of God*, for they are folly to him, and *he is not able to under-stand them because they are spiritually discerned.* The spiri-tual person judges all things, but is himself to be judged by no one. "For who has understood the mind of the Lord so as to instruct him?" But we have the mind of Christ. (1 Corinthians 2:14–16)

We see two things here in our passage:

1. The unsaved (natural) mind is unwilling to accept the things of God because he thinks they are stupid and not essential to his existence or well-being (v. 14a).

2. The unbeliever is unwilling to grasp and embrace spiritual truth and is unable to do so because he does not have the spiritual capability (v. 14b).

Comfort and Clarity.

These two observations provide us with clarity. These things should enlighten us, encourage us, and, to one extent or another, discourage us (all at the same time). They enlighten us because they help us to under-stand why our unsaved loved one is so hard-headed and "bulletproof" when it comes to the gospel (1 Corinthians 2:14). These things should encourage us because we understand that someone else's salvation does not depend upon us or the skill of our presentation of the gospel. In many churches, we are told that if we get the recipe right, people will "get saved" or "ask Jesus into their hearts." Nothing could be further from the truth. 1 Corinthians 2:14 can discourage us because we may come to understand that we may never live to see a loved one come to Christ. However, the discouragement shouldn't last because the genuine issue is the power of God, not our persuasion, in terms of salvation.

Nothing New.

It has always been this way. From the Old Testament to the New Testament, the Holy Spirit has always jump-started our spiritual heart or applied God's "paddles" to a dead heart. God explains this through the prophet Ezekiel in what comes across like more of a heart transplant!

> And *I will give you a new heart,* and a new spirit I will put within you. And *I will remove the heart of stone* from your flesh *and give you a heart of flesh.* And *I will put my Spirit within you, and cause you to walk* in my statutes and be careful to obey my rules. (Ezekiel 36:26–27)

Notice the work of the Spirit. Notice the work of God to "restart" or "transplant" a new heart. That's regeneration. We are a new creation (2 Corinthians 5:17). God regenerates our dead hearts. The regenerated human heart changes from stone, dead and cold, to flesh, alive and coursing with spiritual life. We now hear and can respond to the Gospel, resulting in our salvation and the indwelling power of the Holy Spirit!

NEEDED AND NECESSARY

Until regeneration occurs, the unbeliever's mind remains blinded to the truth. They cannot "see" the truth because they do not want to see the truth. Why not? The enemy has blinded their minds; their spiritual eyes do not see the truth.

> In their case *the god of this world has blinded the minds of the unbelievers, to keep them from* seeing the light of the gospel of the glory of Christ, who is the image of God. (2 Corinthians 4:4)

They are like starving lions in a cage piled high with soy protein, staring at a bowl of red meat just out of reach. Soy would provide life-saving protein. However, the lion has no appetite or desire for soy protein. In the same way, the unsaved have no appetite for salvation. Their ears and minds (and appetites) are inclined elsewhere. They do not want the truth because every intention of their heart leans toward evil. That is the state of the natural man who has not had a supernatural encounter with God. It's been that way since the fall of mankind in the Garden of Eden. It was that kind of evil that brought about Noah's flood.

> The LORD saw that the wickedness of man was great in the earth, and that *every intention of the thoughts of his heart was only evil continually.* (Genesis 6:5)

Humanity, apart from the Spirit's intervention and regeneration, has inherited "original sin" and passes it on in his spiritual "genetic code." We are born dead in our sins and trespasses (Ephesians 2:1–5). Even when we embrace the Savior, we pass this sin problem on to our children. It's no wonder that we read right after the flood that this problem remained.

And when the LORD smelled the pleasing aroma, the LORD said in his heart, "I will never again curse the ground because of man, *for the intention of man's heart is evil from his youth.* Neither will I ever again strike down every living creature as I have done. (Genesis 8:21)

Divine Intervention Required.

The fallen mind hungers for evil, not for good. The fallen conscience is bent toward evil from its earliest conscious moments through its most mature adult state. It pursues evil. Because the unsaved mind cannot appreciate the goodness and grace of God, it has no yearning or hunger for God:

> as it is written: "*None is righteous, no, not one*; no one understands; *no one seeks for God.* All have turned aside; together they have become worthless; no one does good, not even one... *There is no fear of God before their eyes.*" (Romans 3:10–12, 18)

Uninterested in its Creator, the fallen mind lives out its days without considering what is just, right, and pleasing to the God it seeks to ignore.

Insanity.

It's as if the fallen mind is crazy. It is! The blindness of the fallen mind produces an imbalance in our moral faculties bordering on insanity at times. Therefore, we need divine intervention before regeneration and salvation. Apart from Divine Intervention (regeneration), this is a chronic and terminal spiritual condition. It is indeed like we are insane:

> This is an evil in all that is done under the sun, that the same event happens to all. *Also, the hearts of the children of man are*

full of evil, and madness is in their hearts while they live, and after that they go to the dead. (Ecclesiastes 9:3)

Unwilling and Unable.

For the mind that is set on the flesh is hostile to God, for it does not submit to God's law; indeed, it cannot. (Romans 8:7)

Theirs is a moral compass and conscience that cannot function properly. Theirs is a moral compass that is unable and unwilling to do rightly as it lacks the ability and desire to do so in its fallen (unregenerate) state. It cannot change course, and it cannot change what it is. This kind of change of nature requires divine intervention, a miracle of divine grace. The prophet Jeremiah illustrates for us the dilemma of those who are spiritually dead (unregenerate):

Can the Ethiopian change his skin or the leopard his spots? Then also you can do good who are accustomed to do evil. (Jeremiah 13:23)

This reminds us that the Spirit gives life and the flesh is no good at all (John 6:63). The moral compass of a fallen mind is broken. The heart, apart from the regenerating work of the Holy Spirit, is desperately wicked (Jeremiah 17:9). People, apart from the work of the Spirit, are unwilling to come to Christ for salvation. You see this in the teaching of the Lord Jesus in John 5:39–40:

You search the Scriptures because you think that in them you have eternal life; and it is they that bear witness about me, yet *you refuse to come to me that you may have life.*

Spiritual Blindness, Spiritual Hostility

The Holy Spirit tells us through the pen of the Apostle Paul that the unbeliever (apart from the Spirit's work) has a conscience that is seared (1 Timothy 4:2).

IGNORANCE NO EXCUSE

Let's not kid ourselves. Rejecting God isn't because of a lack of revelation. God has revealed himself to all people through all that he has made. He has made himself known through his word. He has revealed himself in the person and work of Jesus Christ. Regrettably, people repress and suppress this awareness. How can we be so sure? Paul's writing in Romans makes this sad reality clear:

> For the wrath of God is revealed from heaven against all ungodliness and unrighteousness of men, *who by their unrighteousness suppress the truth.* For what can be known about God is plain to them, because *God has shown it to them.* For his invisible attributes, namely, his eternal power and divine nature, have been clearly perceived, ever since the creation of the world, in the things that have been made. *So they are without excuse. For although they knew God, they did not honor him as God or give thanks to him,* but they became futile in their thinking, and their foolish hearts were darkened. (Romans 1:18–21)

Divine Intervention Always Required!

The Spirit gives life to the dead and deadened heart (John 6:63). It is the Holy Spirit that first performs a spiritual heart transplant (Ezekiel 36:26–27). Apart from the divine intervention to "shock our hearts," our spiritual hearts are dead to God, unwilling and therefore unable to come to him.

More Than an Explanation

If it was simply a matter of a good explanation, or if "seeing was believing," then Judas Iscariot, after three years with Jesus, would have embraced Christ and refused to betray him. But we know that is not the case. It's not a matter of ignorance. It's a matter of stubborn refusal. That's why the Holy Spirit, God, not men, does the work (men are merely the harvesters). God gives us a new heart, putting his Spirit within us, and then we respond. From then on out, we are new creations (2 Corinthians 5:17). We now understand the things of God, our spiritual state, and our need for a Savior because our minds are no longer darkened but enlightened:

> The *natural person does not accept the things of the Spirit of God, for they are folly to him,* and he is not able to understand them because they are spiritually discerned. The spiritual person judges all things, but is himself to be judged by no one. "For who has understood the mind of the Lord so as to instruct him?" But *we have the mind of Christ.* (1 Corinthians 2:14–16)

The Spirit's Work

What's this got to do with people "getting saved?" As we noted already, no one comes to Christ without the Spirit's regenerating their heart. Salvation begins with divine intervention by the Holy Spirit. He regenerates our hearts, we see our condition, and we recognize we need a Savior, and we really want THE Savior. We surrender. If we had to sequence this in human terms, it would sequence something like this:[4]

---

4   Many systematic theologies go into greater detail by providing more steps; however, for our purposes, we offer a simplified description.

1. **Regeneration:** God the Holy Spirit brings the heart to life.

2. **Conversion:** Once dead to God, the regenerated heart exercises saving faith expressed through a repentant heart that turns from sin to confidence in God and his promises.

3. **Salvation:** God forgives and justifies our sins, declaring us forgiven once and for all.

This sequence can happen in seconds, minutes, or hours—in some cases, years. However, it always results in salvation. A regenerated person cannot later become unsaved. Regeneration happens before salvation. Growth comes afterward. It, too, is the work of the Holy Spirit, as he leads us into all truth, uses us to convince the world concerning sin, righteousness, and judgment, and brings to mind all we have learned through the Scriptures. Regeneration is the work of the Spirit where he sparks spiritual life into the dead heart of the unbeliever so that the unbeliever can hear and comprehend the gospel. Regeneration ends in salvation. It is the work of the Spirit upon which all depends.

SIDE EFFECTS: ILLUMINATION

Illumination?

You may recall that we mentioned "illumination" in chapter one. Illumination comes after salvation. It is a "side effect" of our salvation and the indwelling of the Holy Spirit (John 14:26). Illumination is part of how the Holy Spirit, as our Helper, leads us into all truth. In illumination, the Holy Spirit causes "the light to go on" in the believer's mind, enabling him to grasp the things of God more fully. Both regeneration and illumination are of utmost importance in the primary mission of the Holy Spirit. They are how the Holy Spirit guides God's people into truth, bringing to mind what they have read from the Word of God.

Not Revelation.

Don't confuse illumination with revelation. They are in some ways similar and yet very different. But looking at the root words, you sense the difference. Illumination is from the word illuminate. That speaks of light. Revelation is from the word reveal. This speaks of something different. Sure, light reveals things, but it's not the same thing. Revelation occurred when God told (or uncovered) new truth to the prophets and apostles as they wrote Scripture, or in the case of non-writing prophets, spoke God's word to others (like Elijah rebuking King Ahab).

Sometimes, illumination may feel like God has spoken a new revelation to us. But don't be confused (or deceived). We already have sufficient revelation because we have the entire Bible. God, the Holy Spirit, illuminates what we have read and studied to lead and help us. The Holy Spirit leads us into all truth by causing "the light to go on" in an "aha!" spiritual moment. What happens is this. We see the matter in a new, clearer light (i.e., illumination). We see illumination demonstrated by the Spirit's granting the Apostle Peter wisdom for the selection of a new apostle, Matthias:

> In those days Peter stood up among the brothers (the company of persons was in all about 120) and said, "Brothers, *the Scriptures had to be fulfilled, which the Holy Spirit spoke beforehand* by the mouth of David concerning Judas, who became a guide to those who arrested Jesus. For he was numbered among us and was allotted his share in this ministry." (Now this man acquired a field with the reward of his wickedness, and falling headlong he burst open in the middle and all his bowels gushed out. And it became known to all the inhabitants of Jerusalem, so that the field was called in their own language Akeldama, that is, Field of Blood.) *"For it is written in the Book of Psalms, 'May his camp become desolate, and let*

there be no one to dwell in it'; and 'Let another take his office.'"
(Acts 1:15–20)

Peter did not receive a new revelation. Peter received illumination
(greater understanding). The Holy Spirit illuminated Peter's heart and
mind, providing greater understanding based on what had already been
revealed in the Scriptures. This was done so that the Apostles could
replace Judas. This is an example of illumination. God brought to mind
with new clarity something they already knew (John 14:26). By the
illumination of the Spirit, they understood and applied God's Word in a
more complete way to a particular situation. You may have experienced
something similar when you observed and understood something in a
text you read many times before.

Illumination a Gift.

Illumination is also a gift of the Spirit. It is not a gift in what we usu-
ally consider "spiritual gifts." Not everyone receives every spiritual gift
(1 Corinthians 12:27–30). However, everyone experiences illumination.[5] As believers, we receive illumination through the indwelling power
of the Holy Spirit we experience.

REVIEW AND REMEMBER

Salvation and Regeneration.

Regeneration is the work of the Spirit where he sparks spiritual life into
the dead heart of the unbeliever so that the unbeliever is made alive to the
things of God. This is essential to our salvation. Regeneration jumpstarts
new life in a dead heart. The Holy Spirit does this so that we hear, understand, and embrace the gospel. Regeneration always ends in salvation.

---

5   We will deal with the distribution of gifts in greater detail later, as well as other ways the
     Spirit empowers and aids believers.

Salvation and Illumination.

Illumination comes after salvation. Through illumination, the Holy Spirit causes "the light to go on" in the believer's mind, enabling him to grasp the things of God more fully. Both regeneration and illumination play a vital role in fulfilling the primary mission of the Holy Spirit. They are essential to his leading us into all truth and bringing to mind all we have learned of Jesus' teachings.

APPLICATION

Be Thankful!

Thank God that regeneration and salvation depend upon him and not us. Evangelize like it depends on you and sleep at night as if it depends on him. Be thankful and rejoice that no one's salvation depends on you and me, the mood we create, our techniques, or our actions (John 6:63; 1:12–13).

Be Confident!

Abide in Christ, keep his Word, and let the Holy Spirit do the heavy lifting. Be confident that God will accomplish in you the plans he has for you and your ministry. Be faithful, knowing God will accomplish what he purposes (Philippians 2:12–13).

Be at Peace!

Do not lose heart. Do not be discouraged. Share the gospel the best you can. Don't be afraid. One plants; one waters; another harvests; God provides the increase. Strive to be faithful (1 Corinthians 3:6–9).

Understand!

When you evangelize others, understand what you are up against dead people! Dead people don't respond to lifeguards. You can present the gospel all day long, calling people to repentance. Unless the Spirit is regenerating their heart, they will not respond. The natural (unsaved; unchurched) man cannot understand the things of God because they are folly to him (1 Corinthians 2:14).

Pray for illumination!

Ask God to help you understand his complete revelation of himself to mankind (the Bible). God has given you all you need. You have his Spirit, his word, and his church. Pray for illumination (Psalm 119:18; John 14:26).

FOR FURTHER THOUGHT

1. Have you ever watched a television show where doctors applied defibrillating paddles to a patient to restart a stopped heart? Have you ever seen an episode where a dead or unconscious patient applied those paddles to himself or herself? Apply this to the Holy Spirit's work in regeneration and salvation. Relate this to John 6:63 and Ezekiel 36:26–27.

2. How do regeneration and salvation apply to Ephesians 2:1–5 and Colossians 2:13? How might this all relate to jumper cables or the paddles we discussed in question 1?

3. Think back over what you have read in this chapter. How has illumination factored into this? Has it?

4. Re-read Acts 1:15–20. Ask God to illumine your understanding of this passage where illumination is demonstrated. Read Psalm 119:18. How is David asking for illumination? How can you do the same?

5. Using "root words," explain the difference between illumination and revelation in a sentence or two.

5

THE HOLY SPIRIT
AND YOUR
SPIRITUAL GIFTS

Now concerning spiritual gifts, brothers,
I do not want you to be uninformed.
(1 Corinthians 12:1)

Human beings are creatures of extremes. We said this earlier. As is often the case regarding "controversial issues," any discussion of spiritual gifts can become polarizing. Regrettably, such discussions can resemble today's political landscape more than they do a landscape dotted and populated by Christ-followers. Since the Church is comprised of different people from every tongue, tribe, people, and nation, we must remember that as different as all true believers might be or appear, we are related by blood—the shed blood of Jesus Christ. We should not take division in the body of Christ lightly. As I've mentioned before, this book is neither pro-charismatic nor anti-charismatic. It is pro-God and pro-Bible. Therefore, let us reason together from the Bible and see what the Holy Spirit says about himself and "spiritual gifts."

ASKING THE RIGHT QUESTIONS

Have the Gifts Ceased?
While many people would like to focus on the non-continuation or continuation of the gifts today, we will do better. We will develop a foundational understanding of how gifts operate and are to be deployed from the biblical point of view that is grounded in the text of Scripture. Let's start with the basics.

Who Gives, Who Receives?
Who gives the gifts and to whom (and how do we know)? We return to the essential question for settling all such matters. What does the Bible say? Let's get the fundamentals straight, laying the groundwork for further discussions and exploration. 1 Corinthians 12–14 provides us great insight into spiritual gifts and the Holy Spirit's distribution and will for their use. The Holy Spirit says through the Apostle Paul:

> Now there are varieties of gifts, but the same Spirit; and there are varieties of service, but the same Lord; and there are varieties of activities, but *it is the same God who empowers them all in everyone. To each is given the manifestation of the Spirit for the common good.* For to one is given through the Spirit the utterance of wisdom, and to another the utterance of knowledge according to the same Spirit, to another faith by the same Spirit, to another gifts of healing by the one Spirit, to another the working of miracles, to another prophecy, to another the ability to distinguish between spirits, to another various kinds of tongues, to another the interpretation of tongues. All these are empowered by one and the same Spirit, who apportions to each one individually *as he wills.* (1 Corinthians 12:4–11)

And the Giver Is.

The Holy Spirit gives "spiritual gifts" as he wills (1 Corinthians 12:11). The Word of God tells us that the Holy Spirit is the Giver of spiritual gifts (vv. 7–8). "To each is given a manifestation of the Spirit for the common good" (v. 7). The Holy Spirit is the Giver of the "gifts of the Spirit." Everyone who receives a spiritual gift receives that gift from the Holy Spirit for a specific end and purpose, according to his will. And his will is found in the Scriptures. Some may disagree, but we value Scripture over preference. The Scriptures are the revelation made more sure as the Word of God (2 Peter 1:19–21).

The Recipients Are.

To whom are the gifts given? The gifts, as the context of our passage shows, are presented to those within the Church. Only believers receive the so-called "spiritual gifts" or "gifts of the spirit." The Holy Spirit writes:

> All these are empowered by one and the same Spirit, who apportions to each one individually as he wills. For just as the body is one and has many members, and all the members of the body, though many, are one body, so it is with Christ. For in one Spirit we were all baptized into one body—Jews or Greeks, slaves or free—and all were made to drink of one Spirit. For the body does not consist of one member but of many. If the foot should say, "Because I am not a hand, I do not belong to the body," that would not make it any less a part of the body. And if the ear should say, "Because I am not an eye, I do not belong to the body," that would not make it any less a part of the body. If the whole body were an eye, where would be the sense of hearing? If the whole body were an ear, where would be the sense of smell? But as it is, God arranged the members in the body, each one of them, as he chose. (1 Corinthians 12:11–18)

Here, we see that members of the body of Christ are the recipients of the spiritual gifts (v. 12). The flow of the passage shows that regardless of nationality or race, all true Christians receive whatever spiritual gifts they have from the Holy Spirit (vv. 11, 18). Only a born-again Christian can receive a spiritual gift. Others may display "counterfeit gifts;" however, if they are not in Christ, then their gift is counterfeit (1 Corinthians 12:3). For example, Hindus, Muslims, and Mormons "speak in tongues." They are not Christians. Whatever they are doing, it is not from God the Holy Spirit (2 Corinthians 11:4). They are idolaters worshipping other gods. This leads us to the following question.

On What Basis.

How is the distribution of gifts determined, and by whom? Don't be put off by seemingly basic questions. Such questions are fundamental to correctly understanding the gifts of the Holy Spirit. Let's remember what we have learned already. The Holy Spirit's goal is to bring glory not to Himself but to God the Son: "But when the Helper comes, whom I will send to you from the Father, the Spirit of truth, who proceeds from the Father, he will bear witness about me" (John 15:26). The Holy Spirit's mission is to bring glory and attention and honor to Jesus, not himself: "When the Spirit of truth comes, he will guide you into all the truth, for he will not speak on his own authority, but whatever he hears he will speak, and he will declare to you the things that are to come. He will glorify me, for he will take what is mine and declare it to you" (John 16:13–14). This reality challenges many popular misconceptions and notions about spiritual gifts and "gifted" persons.

God's Anointed?

As a new believer, I attended a large church in central Florida pastored by a man who often described himself (and allowed others to describe him) as "God's anointed." The idea was that he was somehow very special because he was very gifted and that he was very gifted because he was very special.

There is a tendency these days for so-called "gifted" men and women to allow themselves to be designated as "God's anointed." These individuals mistakenly accept (or invite) such honor and are often put on a pedestal for their apparent giftedness. The assumption is that they must be, crass as it sounds, "especially special" because God has given great spiritual and supernatural gifts to them. Nothing could be further from the truth. If you stop and think about it, God does not save us because we are deserving or special.

Think about it. God blesses us with salvation not because of works but because of grace. And what is grace? Grace is God's undeserved favor. We are all sinners (Romans 3:23). God saves us despite who and how we are (Romans 6:23). No one deserves anything remotely resembling the attention and devotion servants of Christ show God. We are just servants. Jesus taught servants are not accorded special honor because they deserve none:

> Will any one of you who has a servant plowing or keeping
> sheep say to him when he has come in from the field, 'Come
> at once and recline at table'? Will he not rather say to him,
> 'Prepare supper for me, and dress properly, and serve me
> while I eat and drink, and afterward you will eat and drink'?
> *Does he thank the servant because he did what was commanded?*
> So you also, *when you have done all that you were commanded,
> say, "We are unworthy servants; we have only done what was
> our duty."* (Luke 17:7–10)

None are Special, No Not One!
The unruly church at Corinth had prideful people who insisted they were special. At best, they could only say, as Jesus says above, "We have only

done our duty" (Luke 17:10). At worst, they were reckless and disobedient. Paul bluntly reminded these gifted individuals that they were not unique or deserving of special honor. Therefore, the Holy Spirit moved Paul to write and scold them for their factionalism and pride.

> For who sees anything different in you? What do you have that you did not receive? If then you received it, why do you boast as if you did not receive it? (1 Corinthians 4:7)

Like many of the Christians in Corinth, some Christians today engage in a confused line of reasoning. They mistakenly believe that the Holy Spirit distributes gifts to deserving or unique people. We are told something like, "Hey… these people are special or spiritually superior. They are God's anointed." This flies in the face of what Jesus teaches us in Luke 17:7–10. It contradicts what the Spirit moved Paul to write to prideful and misguided Christians in Corinth in 1 Corinthians 4:7.[6] Those who accept such praise are misguided. This kind of thinking is the very thinking the Holy Spirit confronted in the unruly church at Corinth: "For who sees anything different in you? What do you have that you did not receive? If then you received it, why do you boast as if you did not receive it" (1 Corinthians 4:7)?

Many of the "gifted" people at Corinth had mistakenly believed they were special. They became haughty and arrogant. The Holy Spirit rebuked them through his apostle. The Bible teaches us that God's power is displayed in our weakness, not our worthiness (2 Corinthians 12:7–10). We are all undeserving of the ultimate and greatest gift—our salvation—or any other spiritual gift. This reality leads us to consider the next question.

---

6   A better translation of 1 Corinthians 4:7 reads: "For who regards you as superior? What do you have that you did not receive? And if you did receive it, why do you boast as if you had not received it?" (NASB).

Why and How?

Why do we receive our spiritual gifts, and how? We've asked and answered this question, to some extent, already. Let's consider it from another angle. What does the Bible say about the giving of gifts by the Holy Spirit? We find the Holy Spirit's answer to these questions in 1 Corinthians 12:1–18, excerpted below.

> Now concerning spiritual gifts, brothers, I do not want you to be uninformed.... Now there are varieties of gifts, but the same Spirit; and there are varieties of service, but the same Lord; and there are varieties of activities, but it is the same God who empowers them all in everyone. To each is given the manifestation of the Spirit for the common good. (1 Corinthians 12:1, 4–7)

God the Holy Spirit distributes spiritual gifts to individual believers in whatever number he determines for the sake of the whole church, "the common good." God does not intend to glorify individuals. The Holy Spirit's mission is to glorify Christ (John 16:14). What gift you receive is determined by God for the sake of the larger body of Christ (i.e., "the common good"). God shares his glory with no human being. We only have what we receive and should not regard ourselves as special or superior to anyone or anything (1 Corinthians 4:7). At best, we only do our duty—what is expected of us as good slaves (Luke 17:10).

God Decides, Not Us.

Through the pen of the Apostle Paul, the Holy Spirit states that God decides what gifts we get and the extent of their power. Even a cursory reading of the text indicates gifts are distributed not according to the individual's worthiness or 'special-ness' but according to God's will. No individual person, no part of the body of Christ, is more important than another. Each member of the body of Christ, with whatever gift they

have, is just as vital to the mission and ministry of the Church as any
other. We, with our gifts, all constitute the body of Christ.

> All these are empowered by one and the same Spirit, *who*
> *apportions to each one individually as he wills.* For just as the
> body is one and has many members, and all the members
> of the body, though many, are one body, so it is with Christ.
> For in one Spirit we were all baptized into one body—Jews
> or Greeks, slaves, or free—and all were made to drink of one
> Spirit. For the body does not consist of one member but of
> many. If the foot should say, "Because I am not a hand, I do
> not belong to the body," that would not make it any less a
> part of the body. And if the ear should say, "Because I am not
> an eye, I do not belong to the body," that would not make it
> any less a part of the body. If the whole body were an eye,
> where would be the sense of hearing? If the whole body
> were an ear, where would be the sense of smell? *But as it is,*
> *God arranged the members in the body, each one of them, as he*
> *chose.* (1 Corinthians 12:11–18)

God determines "who gets what" in terms of spiritual gifts as he wills
(v. 11). Each member of the body needs and depends upon the others
and their gifts as different as each person and each gift might be (vv. 13,
17). "God arranged the members of the body, each one of them, as he
chose" (v. 18). To this extent, we are all God's anointed in that we have
all received whatever gift we have from him through the Spirit and none
of us are "more special" or more deserving than the other.

APPLICATION

You may be at a crossroads. I ask you to prayerfully consider two courses of action.

Recognize a need to carefully evaluate what you believe. Want what God wants. We come back to the questions we said we would ask earlier as we looked for answers. Let these be your application and matters for further thought.

FOR FURTHER THOUGHT

1. As I consider (reconsider) my understanding of the Holy Spirit, am I willing to go not where my tradition, church, or family has taken me but where the Scriptures take me? What does the text say, what do the words mean, and how then shall I think and live?

2. Will I trust the clear, natural, and commonsensical reading of the text or will I read into the text?

PART THREE

CONTROVERSIES

6

SPIRITUAL GIFTS AND DESIGNER SPECIFICATIONS

God is spirit, and those who worship him must
worship in spirit and truth. (John 4:24)

G od is the Creator of all things, and he made them very good (cf. Genesis 1:1, 31) God created all that is. He has made everything according to its time (Ecclesiastes 3:11). As Creator, God is also the Designer. Consequently, God knows why he made what he made and their purpose. Moreover, God, like a design engineer, knows and understands the tolerances (limits) of the things he created, even people (cf. 1 Corinthians 10:13).

God, our Creator-Designer, comprehensively and perfectly knows what humans can endure. He understands our limits. The psalmist writes "For he knows our frame; he remembers that we are dust" (Psalm 103:14). God is our designer and like every excellent designer, with every good design, he built us according to his "designer specifications." Wikipedia tells us that a designer specification "may also give specific examples of how the design should be executed, helping others work properly (a guideline for what the person should do)."[7] In similar fashion, God gave us specifications for using our spiritual gifts.

Everything has One

When you think about it, everything has "designer specifications" stipulating what we are and are not to do with a product. There are designer specifications prescribing how often you should change the oil in your car. The manufacturer tells you what gasoline is best for your motor, down to the prescribed octane rating. Household appliances come with designer specifications and or rules for use. We have a new coffee grinder, and the manufacturer tells us we are not to grind for more than two minutes at a time. If we exceed the designer's specifications, the grinder will shut down for 30 minutes. Everything comes with operating instructions, prescriptions, and specifications for use. Violate these specifications, and you may invalidate or damage a product's warranty. Believe it or not, the same applies to spiritual gifts.

God's Rules, God Rules.

Our "operating manual" is the Bible. It gives us God's specifications for everything. It tells us everything we need to know for life, faith, and practice (2 Timothy 3:16–17). Exodus 20:3–17 and Deuteronomy 5:7–21 provide us with "10 rules for life," also known as "The Ten Commandments." God gave us these specifications so that, among other things, we could enjoy a moral and well-ordered society.

God has provided us specifications for healthy family relationships— "children obey your parents" (Ephesians 6:1)—and he has given us "specs" for a loving marital relationship—"Husbands love your wives as Christ loved the church" (Ephesians 5:25). God reveals such things to

---

7   Wikipedia contributors, "Design specification," *Wikipedia, The Free Encyclopedia*, July 17, 2025, https://en.wikipedia.org/w/index.php?title=Design_specification&oldid=1300926728.

us through his operating manual, the Bible: "Believe in the Lord Jesus and you will be saved" (Acts 16:31). Call these principles and practices "Designer Specifications." God is the Designer. He knows why things are, how things work, and how to maintain them best. He understands our strengths, our weaknesses, and our tolerances. Our good and loving God wants what's best for us. And so he has told us how to use our spiritual gifts.

Look Around You!
Evidences of God's rules (and his reign) are everywhere. You see them in the way the world functions and operates. The Sun rises and sets "on time." We fall down, but we never "fall up." He's decreed the law of gravity. God has rules. He is a God of order.

God is very particular about how things are done. As the one who made everything, he knows best. He knows what his purposes were in creating all things. That's why there is a right and wrong way to do everything (according to specifications). Violate his prescriptions at your peril. That's one reason he tells us in Romans 6:23, "The wages of sin is death …."

God has a purpose and prescription for every gift and everything he has given us. He's the Great Physician who prescribes. As his patients, we should take what he prescribes as directed. We do well to follow his directions. He is, after all, God. This applies to the gifts of the Spirit.

"SPECS" FOR SPIRITUAL GIFTS

Believe it or not, clear-cut designer specifications exist for using our spiritual gifts. The first one we see is: "To each is given the manifestation of the Spirit for the common good" (1 Corinthians 12:7). He gives us whatever gifts we have for the common good of the Church, rather than personal use. We employ our gifts for the good of all, not for ourselves or our benefit. When we employ them for some other reason, we sin. This may sound harsh but sin is doing something outside God's will. If we love God then we will keep his commands because they are not burdensome to us (John 14:15; 1 John 5:3).

Use as Directed.

The Holy Spirit tells us through the pen of the Apostle Paul that our spiritual gifts are to be used according to God's specifications. They are not ours to use as we please. As we already discussed, they are to be used for the common good and not for personal gain or benefit (1 Corinthians 12:7). He distributes the gifts to whom he wills as he chooses, in whatever quantity he ordained.

> All these are empowered by one and the same Spirit, who *apportions to each one individually as he wills*... If the whole body were an eye, where would be the sense of hearing? If the whole body were an ear, where would be the sense of smell? But as it is, God arranged the members in the body, *each one of them, as he chose.* (1 Corinthians 12:11, 17–18)

Some feel they can do what they want (when they want) with their spiritual gifts. The problem is the word "feel." Too many people talk about their feelings and ignore the designer specifications and prescriptions written by the Great Physician in the God-breathed Scriptures.

Feelings Change Frequently.

Even as Christians, our feelings often change. They ebb and flow like the tides. They often change like the weather. There's an old saying: "Don't like the weather? Wait fifteen minutes, and it'll change." Our feelings may change or deceive us. God's word never changes or expires (1 Peter 1:22–25).

God's Unchanging Word.

As we've discussed already, human beings are creatures of extremes. Moreover, human beings dislike being bound or restricted by God's Word. God never changes (Micah 3:6; Hebrews 13:8). Like him, his Word never changes (1 Peter 1:25; Isaiah 40:8). Because God never changes and because God's Word never changes, we look to his Word for direction. As we will see, God's specifications were a problem for many in Paul's day. It's a problem today for many professing Christians. Why would this be a problem for so many?

Pride One Problem.

Paul wrote to the unruly church at Corinth about their prideful and sinful conduct. They acted like they were special because of their intelligence, because of their wealth, and because of their God-given (unearned) spiritual gifts. Paul warns them: "For who regards you as superior? What do you have that you did not receive? And if you did receive it, why do you boast as if you had not received it" (1 Corinthians 4:7 [NASB])? The unruly Church of Corinth acted as if they had earned their salvation. They often acted as if they deserved the gifts God bestowed. They acted as if their gifts made them special when their unearned gifts were granted for the glory of God and the good of others.

SPECIFICATIONS SPECIFIED

Interdependence.

All spiritual gifts, whatever they are (sign gifts or ministerial gifts), are to be used for the common good (1 Corinthians 12:7). God designed the various parts of the body of Christ to work interdependently, not independently.

> For the body does not consist of one member but of many.
> If the foot should say, "Because I am not a hand, I do not

> belong to the body," that would not make it any less a part
> of the body.... But as it is, God arranged the members in the
> body, each one of them, as he chose. If all were a single mem-
> ber, where would the body be? As it is, there are many parts,
> yet one body. (1 Corinthians 12:14–15, 18–20)

The body of Christ, the church, is just that, a body made up of different members or body parts. Each serves its purpose as part of the greater whole. Each serves the common good (1 Corinthians 12:7). These individual parts work interdependently for the common good. The Holy Spirit reminds us elsewhere that we are members of one another.

> *So we, though many, are one body in Christ, and individually*
> *members one of another.* Having gifts that differ according to
> the grace given to us, let us use them.... (Romans 12:5–6)

Thus, the Holy Spirit employs all these body-part word pictures throughout the New Testament in 1 Corinthians 12:17–21 and Romans 12:4–8 to show interdependence. Where would a foot be without a hand and where would the body be?

Every gift and gifted person is interdependent, like the Trinity. The Holy Spirit's mission and ministry is to "operate in the background" as part of the Trinity, each member having his role. Likewise, those to whom the Holy Spirit distributes gifts are to remain in the background, bringing glory to Christ rather than to themselves. They are to make much of Christ for the common good. In doing this, the Spirit gives certain people a particular gift. No two people in a church necessarily receive the same gift or gift set (1 Corinthians 12:27–31). Because no believer in your church gets the same gifts, they must depend on one another (1 Corinthians 12:4–11). They must use their spiritual gifts interdependently. Indeed, some gifts are more prominent looking, while others appear less important (1 Corinthians 12:28, 31). Nevertheless, all body parts are essential. God has precise specifications for them all.

Deployed with Precision.

Due to space limitations, we are unable to discuss how all the gifts should be employed individually. Rather than discussing all the gifts, let's discuss designer specifications for a greater (ministry) gift and a lesser (miraculous) gift. The Holy Spirit provides us with side-by-side examples of two such gifts with his prescriptions:

> *Let all things be done for edification.* If anyone speaks in a tongue, *it should be by two or at the most three, and each in turn, and one must interpret;* but if there is no interpreter, he must keep silent in the church; and let him speak to himself and God. *Let two or three prophets speak, and let the others pass judgment.* But if a revelation is made to another who is seated, the first one must keep silent. For you can all *prophesy one by one, so that all may learn and all may be exhorted;* and the spirits of prophets are subject to prophets; *for God is not a God of confusion but of peace, as in all the churches of the saints.* (1 Corinthians 14:26–33 [NASB])

Just as there is an appropriate way to maintain your car (according to the manufacturer's specifications) and take medicine (according to prescription), there is a right and wrong way to use God's gifts. They say, "the devil is in the details." But I think God is in the details, and the enemy wants to confuse these details.

The Details.

The Holy Spirit commanded:

1. We must use a gift for the common good to build others up (v. 26).

2.   In Corinth, individuals with the gift of tongues were instructed to speak one at a time, and the maximum number of speakers in a worship gathering was limited to three. They were only to speak if they knew an interpreter to be present (vv. 27–28). Thus says the Lord.

3.   If anyone at Corinth had a prophecy (or teaching), such individuals were to speak one at a time, and not more than three were to speak at a worship gathering. Their prophecy or teaching was to be scrutinized by prophets (v. 29). So writes the Holy Spirit. Thus says the Lord.

4.   Prophets were to speak with self-control (a fruit of the Spirit) because the spirit of the prophet was under control by the prophet (vv. 30–32). This is the word of God.

5.   These commands are applied across the board to all Christian churches (v. 33). This is what the God-breathed Scriptures teach.

6.   The rationale was that the churches should be like the orderly God they worship (v. 33). This is God's revealed will.

Disobey at Your Peril.

The "let" words in our English translations are often "command markers," showing us that these statements are commands of God (imperatives), not suggestions. They communicate the imperative mood stated in the original language. These statements are commands to be obeyed, not disobeyed.[8] Paul is reining in the chaotic behaviors of the unruly church at Corinth. However, we remember that the Holy Spirit writes these commands through Paul "for all churches." The Spirit explicitly says so in 1 Corinthians 14:37–38. The Holy Spirit warns us:

---

8   What do we call it when someone chooses to disobey God? Sin.

> If anyone thinks he is a prophet or spiritual, let him recognize that the things which I write to you are the Lord's commandment. *But if anyone does not recognize this, he is not recognized.* (1 Corinthians 14:37–38 [NASB])

These specifications (commands) seem clear and straightforward. Nevertheless, one can only imagine how some at the unruly church at Corinth, like in many churches today, responded to such specifications and restrictions. We know from reading 1–2 Corinthians that there were people who disputed Paul's Apostleship, implying that Paul's writings were not authoritative (i.e., Scripture). Also, people must have said similar things about Paul to the Apostle Peter, who answered them accordingly:

> And count the patience of our Lord as salvation, just as our beloved brother Paul also wrote to you according to the wisdom given him, as he does in all his letters when he speaks in them of these matters. There are some things in them that are hard to understand, which the ignorant and unstable twist to their own destruction, *as they do the other Scriptures.* (2 Peter 3:15–16)

The Apostle Peter understood and wrote others that Paul's letters were Scripture. Peter understood this. Corinth needed to understand this—and so do you and I. The Holy Spirit's commands and Designer specifications in 1 Corinthians 14 are not to be ignored. They are God-breathed. We do well to worship God according to his Designer specifications. God wants us to worship him in spirit and in truth. The Scriptures provide us plenty of examples of those who did not seek to worship him in spirit and in truth (Cain, Nadab and Abihu, and King Saul).

God's Warning.

The Holy Spirit expected resistance to his commands, particularly from the saints at Corinth. So-called gifted people and prophets would challenge these designer specifications or ignore them altogether, as some do today. But Paul emphatically tells us that this is a command of the Lord. Linger over what the Bible says about those who disobey the command of the Lord in this way:

> If anyone thinks he is a prophet or spiritual, let him recognize that the things which I write to you are the Lord's commandment. *But if anyone does not recognize this, he is not recognized.* (1 Corinthians 14:37–38 [NASB])

We should not recognize those who ignore the Spirit's command as legitimate, credible servants of God. This makes sense because a servant is not greater than his master. And God is (or should be) their Master, as well as ours.

Right Way, Wrong Way.

David, a man after God's own heart, writes, "I have hidden your word in my heart that I might not sin against you" (Psalm 19:11 NIV). The Holy Spirit tells us there is an acceptable way and a sinful way to employ or display our gifts and abilities. There's God's way and another's way. Legitimate and serious servants of Christ, according to the Holy Spirit, will use God's gifts God's way. God's gifts are to be used the way he commands. Just as a pharmacist follows the doctor's prescription and the patient takes as directed, we are to obey God as directed in using our gifts. This is part of the practice of our worship (Romans 12:1–8). Follow God's prescription and take as directed. Use your gifts for the glory of God, the good of others, and your growth. You'll be glad you did.

APPLICATION

Just as there was in Corinth in the past, there is much confusion at present regarding the use of spiritual gifts. God, being a God of order, not confusion, has spoken clearly in the Scriptures about the use and abuse of spiritual gifts. Therefore, consider and embrace these three actions:

Recognize a Love for God.

In a God-loving New Testament church, when people spoke in tongues or prophesied, no more than three people did this in a single service. They did so one at a time. If people speak in tongues or prophesy in your church, they will do so according to the timeless prescriptions provided by the Holy Spirit to use his gifts. To do otherwise is to sin. Obedience, in contrast, is expressing love for God.

Remember Self-control.

Some would suggest that they must cry out when the Spirit moves them. But the Holy Spirit has written in his word that the "spirits of the prophets are subject to the prophets" (1 Corinthians 14:32). Self-control is a fruit of the Spirit. The Spirit says he is a God of peace, not confusion (1 Corinthians 14:33). Exercise Spirit-empowered self-control.

Do All God's Way.

In Romans 12:1–8, a parallel passage about spiritual gifts, we are told not to conform to this world. Our world is a world of extremes. God is a God of order and self-control. His ways are not the world's ways. Therefore, when it comes to spiritual gifts, we must "do God's business God's way." We must recognize that those who refuse to honor God's commands cannot be recognized as ministering according to God's will (1 Corinthians 14:37–38). Disobedience delegitimizes the use of whatever gift is displayed.

FOR FURTHER THOUGHT

1. Does the concept of Designer specifications regarding spiritual gifts and their use surprise you? Should it? God's word is filled with his specifications. If God wants things done decently and in order, why would he not show us the right way to use our gifts?

2. We live in a "get ahead world" where everyone seems out for themselves. But the church is to be different. How would this truth be illustrated using our gifts for "the common good" (1 Corinthians 12:7)?

3. Why would someone's failure to recognize and honor God's commands regarding the use of gifts result in them not being recognized as legitimate servants of God in 1 Corinthians 14:37–38)?

4. Reread this chapter. What should we think of churches and leaders who ignore God's prescriptions in using spiritual gifts?

5. What should we think of churches that encourage people or allow numbers of people to speak in tongues all at once or to prophesy all at once? How should we think of church leaders who do? Pastors?

7

TO BE CONTINUED?

I left Trophimus, who was ill, at Miletus.
(2 Timothy 4:20)

ARE THE GIFTS STILL OPERATIVE?

Regarding "all matters Holy Spirit," perhaps the most hotly debated topic is the durability of spiritual gifts. People often ask the simple question, "Are the gifts for today?" While the shorter answer is yes, the longer answer is more complex and nuanced. It begins with the qualifier, "That depends."

Which Gifts?
Some say there were only sign gifts for the Apostles. The Holy Spirit performed these sign gifts through the Apostles to authenticate the miracle worker as a legitimate messenger of God. There are less sensational gifts that appear almost routine, which some call "ministry gifts." Some suggest that all gifts are operative today. Still, others go further to say that any believer could perform any miracle performed in the Bible today if he or she had enough faith. Another group suggests that only the ministry gifts are operative today. They believe that the sign gifts (i.e., the miraculous gifts) faded and ceased when the last apostles died. So the question becomes: Which gifts are operative? Or, which *kinds of* gifts are

operative? Further complicating things is the reality that not everyone agrees on how many gifts there are or what is and is not a gift.

Kinds of Gifts?

As you read through the New Testament, it becomes clear that the Holy Spirit has certain classes or kinds of gifts. There are at least four lists of gifts. While there is some overlap between these lists, there is no indication that they are exhaustive. Lists appear to be illustrative. This adds to the confusion regarding cessation or non-cessation (non-continuation or continuation). We don't know for sure how many gifts exist. How can anyone know that they all have faded?

In Romans 12:6–8, we find a list of seven gifts:

> Having gifts that differ according to the grace given to us, let us use them: if *prophecy*, in proportion to our faith; if *service*, in our serving; the one who teaches, in his *teaching*; the one who exhorts, in his *exhortation*; the one who contributes, in *generosity*; the one who *leads*, with zeal; the one who does acts of *mercy*, with cheerfulness.

These gifts do not appear miraculous. Many people label them as "ministry gifts." However, in other contexts, the prophecy speaks to a prophetic word given by the Holy Spirit through a prophet or prophets, but prophecy also pertains to written Scripture (2 Peter 1:19–21), complicating classification.

1 Corinthians 12:8–10 lists nine spiritual gifts that appear to be miraculous or decidedly supernatural.

> For to one is given through the Spirit *the utterance of wisdom*, and to another *the utterance of knowledge* according to the

same Spirit, *to another faith* by the same Spirit, to another *gifts of healing* by the one Spirit, to another *the working of miracles*, to another *prophecy*, to another *the ability to distinguish between spirits*, to another *various kinds of tongues*, to another *the interpretation of tongues.*

Given the context of gifts listed, "prophecy," here, is more than preaching. While one cannot and we will not seek to define the gifts found in this list, it is not unreasonable to say they likely fall into the miraculous category. Later in chapter 12, there is another list of eight gifts:

And God has appointed in the church first *apostles*, second *prophets*, third *teachers*, then *miracles*, then *gifts of healing*, *helping*, *administrating*, and *various kinds of tongues*. Are all apostles? Are all prophets? Are all teachers? Do all work miracles? Do all possess gifts of healing? Do all speak with tongues? Do all interpret?

Degrees of Importance?

This listing confuses some because it appears to blend offices, miraculous (sign gifts), and ministry gifts (non-miraculous). We will not attempt to define them here. Note, however, that there is a class of miraculous miracles (not to seem redundant) that is somehow different from what would also seem miraculous: gifts of healing and miraculous gifts of various tongues. It is possible that "prophets" speak to both preaching and prophetic utterances. No one can know for sure. Apostles and prophets could overlap as gifts or offices. One thing is clear from the flow of thought in the passage: there appears to be a ranking of gifts from most important to least important. One cannot help but notice that the greater gifts are associated with teaching and preaching more than the miraculous ones. This provides a lesson in itself, according to some.

But Wait, There's More!

Ephesians 4:11–14 provides us with a list of five spiritual gifts. All appear to be associated with teaching and preaching. One cannot help but notice the emphasis of the gifts in this passage (building up believers to maturity).

> And he gave the *apostles*, the *prophets*, the *evangelists*, the *shepherds* and *teachers*, to equip the saints for the work of ministry, for building up the body of Christ, until we all attain to the unity of the faith and of the knowledge of the Son of God, to mature manhood, to the measure of the stature of the fullness of Christ, so that we may no longer be children, tossed to and fro by the waves and carried about by every wind of doctrine, by human cunning, by craftiness in deceitful schemes. (Ephesians 4:11–14)

These gifts do not appear to be miraculous. Their aim is clearly "equipping the saints" to do the business of the kingdom of God ("the work of ministry"). These teaching or preaching gifts aim to provide a clear, unifying understanding of the Christian faith to the flock and maturing the believer for maximum usefulness to his or her Savior.

There is a final list of spiritual gifts in 1 Peter 4:10–11. It is less clear cut but included here.

> As each has received a gift, use it to serve one another, as good stewards of God's varied grace: *whoever speaks, as one who speaks oracles of God; whoever serves, as one who serves by the strength that God supplies*—in order that in everything God may be glorified through Jesus Christ. To him belong glory and dominion forever and ever. Amen. (1 Peter 4:10–11)

This listing confirms that all gifts serve the common good (1 Corinthians 12:7). It intensifies our understanding that the ministry of the Holy Spirit is not to call attention to Himself but to make much of Christ, glorifying God in Christ (John 16:14).

STILL OPERATIVE?

Is the gift of helps for today? Is the gift of generosity (giving) for today? Would anyone deny the gift of administration is operative today? Few would say no. Unfortunately, there is a tendency to lump all gifts, miraculous and not miraculous, and all miracles into the same pot.

Precision Required

Just as there are tendencies toward the extremes among human beings, including Christians, there is also a tendency toward imprecision and sloppiness. In physics, there is something called entropy, which is often described as the second law of thermodynamics.[9] Some call this the "Murphy's Law" of science. Some illustrate it by the need to clean your room regularly because it won't stay clean on its own. Without energy and great effort, all things and processes fall into some form of decay, going from order to disorder—order to chaos. This seems to happen with humans (and Christian humans) in our reasoning through problems that may be emotionally charged. We paint with broad brush strokes when greater care and precision are needed. We look for opportunities to prove our point, becoming less concerned with facts than proving our point. You see this in the political arena today. Few politicians seem willing to hold an honest conversation and examine the facts. Christians must be different.

---

9   "10 Greatest Ideas in the History of Science," *RealClearScience.com*, June 21, 2013, accessed April 16, 2024, https://www.realclearscience.com/lists/10_greatest_ideas_in_the_history_of_science/entropy_universe_tends_toward_disorder.html.

Working Our Way Forward

Let's start with broader questions and work our way forward, asking ourselves, "What does the Bible say," "What does this mean," and "How then shall we think about these things?" Let's take our first question, and it's a broad one. Are all spiritual gifts and or miraculous works equally important and equally durable? Over the course of time does everyone retain the gifts God granted them? Do gift sets change? Why is this important?

Some Christians argue that if we have enough faith any Christian should be able to perform any miracle found in the Bible. The problem they encounter is that they cannot reproduce any miracle found in the Bible. As I write this, we are in the midst of a COVID-19 "lockdown." Many television miracle workers as early as March 2020 called down judgment on the virus with great faith and demanded the immediate creation of an effective vaccine.[10] As of mid-May, the immediate miracle and judgment have not happened. Similar attempts were made in April to blow the virus away with a hot wind, with a supposed great faith, but to no avail.[11] Such attempts would be an Elijah-like miracle. However, while Elijah was an imperfect man with a nature just like any other man, he was able to do what some today cannot do.

> Elijah was a man with a nature like ours, and he prayed fervently that it might not rain, and for three years and six months it did not rain on the earth. (James 5:17)

---

10   Kenneth Copeland, "Judgment Is Executed on COVID-19," March 30, 2020, by Kenneth Copeland Ministries, YouTube, https://www.youtube.com/watch?v=OSIrQBGfUtw.

11   Kenneth Copeland, "2020 Virtual Victory Campaign (April 2–4): A Supernatural Heat Wave!" April 3, 2020, by Kenneth Copeland Ministries, YouTube, https://www.youtube.com/watch?v=XTX3osKtAbs.

Have Times Changed?

Some would argue that Elijah's ministry is not a ministry for today because Elijah's ministry was to a Baal-worshipping Israel that was threatening the Davidic line. God, using Moses, parted the Red Sea (and drowned a pursuing Egyptian army) before nearly 2 million doubting Israelites, who lacked great faith. So great was their lack of faith that they were on the verge of turning on and killing Moses (Exodus 14:10–14). Moses gave water from a stone in front of his doubters (Exodus 17:5–6). Later, performing such a feat while ignoring "designer specifications," Moses was denied entry into the Promised Land (Numbers 20:8–12).

Some observe that "there is only one Exodus," and that type of miracle will not be repeated on a regular basis by anyone, regardless of their faith. We do not see anyone walking on the water as Jesus did before his confused and terrified disciples who, lacking sufficient faith, assumed they had seen a ghost (Matthew 14:26; Mark 6:49). Yet, Jesus walked on the water and none have repeated this feat since. Jesus raised a little girl from the dead despite being "laughed at" (Matthew 9:24). Jesus raised Lazarus from the dead in front of a largely unbelieving crowd populated by many who were his enemies in John 11. When Jesus asked to be taken to the tomb, even those closest to him doubted, afraid Lazarus' corpse would stink. Jesus raised Lazarus from the dead despite the lack of faith.

> Jesus said, "Take away the stone." Martha, the sister of the dead man, said to him, "Lord, by this time there will be an odor, for he has been dead four days." (John 11:39)

How many times when performing miracles did Jesus remark something to the effect of "you of little faith?" One might observe from the Scriptures that certain classes or kinds of miracles do not seem to take place. One could argue that individuals with specific abilities performed such miracles for particular circumstances at specific moments in redemptive history and that they will not occur again. It's not a matter of having enough faith. After all, Jesus performed many of his miracles in the presence of his enemies and antagonists (i.e., the withered hand healing in Mark 3:1–6). But these miracles are not like the signs, wonders, and miraculous gifts of the Apostles in the early church.

What About Sign Gifts?
No one can deny the Apostles spoke in tongues, regardless of your definition of tongues. This is obvious from what we read in Acts 2:1–13, excerpted below.

> Now there were dwelling in Jerusalem Jews, devout men from every nation under heaven. And at this sound the multitude came together, and they were bewildered, because *each one was hearing them speak in his own language.* And they were amazed and astonished, saying, *"Are not all these who are speaking Galileans? And how is it that we hear, each of us in his own native language?* Parthians and Medes and Elamites and residents of Mesopotamia, Judea and Cappadocia, Pontus and Asia, Phrygia and Pamphylia, Egypt and the parts of Libya belonging to Cyrene, and visitors from Rome, both Jews and proselytes, Cretans and Arabians—*we hear them telling in our own tongues the mighty works of God." And all were amazed and perplexed,* saying to one another, "What does this mean?" *But others mocking said, "They are filled with new wine."* (Acts 2:4–13)

Their Existence Undeniable!
We learn a great deal about tongues and miraculous works from this passage, least of all that men did speak in tongues. We also learn what tongues were and that this miraculous work did not depend on the faith of those present (friends, foes, or neutral parties). No one can deny the

Apostle Paul spoke in tongues. He claimed to speak in tongues with great frequency.

> *I thank God that I speak in tongues more than all of you. Nevertheless, in church I would rather speak five words with my mind in order to instruct others, than ten thousand words in a tongue.* (1 Corinthians 14:18–19)

Gifts of Healing Undeniable.

The Bible tells us that the Apostles performed many miraculous healings. It is clear that they possessed the gift of healing. Paul healed many people of all kinds of afflictions. Acts 19:11–12 documents the amazing extent of Paul's gifts of healing:

> And God was doing extraordinary miracles by the hands of Paul, so that even handkerchiefs or aprons that had touched his skin were carried away to the sick, and their diseases left them and the evil spirits came out of them.

God, the Holy Spirit, empowered Paul to heal by his divine power. Acts 19:11–12 reminds us that the power to heal and the time, means, and place of healing (as was even the case with Elijah) is up to God. That's why we look not to the healer but to God. That's why the Holy Spirit cautions us through the pen of the Apostle Paul to not think more highly of ourselves (or the miracle worker) than we should in Romans 12:3–8.

The Holy Spirit's mission and ministry, like our own, is not to call attention to himself. Instead, he brings glory to Christ (John 16:14). God is sovereign over one's gifts in all cases, including the extent and durability of that gift. The Holy Spirit tells us through his God-breathed Scriptures: "All these are empowered by one and the same Spirit, who apportions to each one individually as he wills" (1 Corinthians 12:11).

Durability?

Are the sign gifts, the miraculous gifts, some gifts, or all gifts durable? What does the Bible say? What does the Holy Spirit tell us through his God-breathed Scriptures? Now we come to a hotly contested "bone of contention" for so many people within the Church. Here is where cooler, more thoughtful heads need to prevail.

Let's start with a basic question. Will there be a time when any of the sign gifts, or miraculous gifts, will cease or fade? What is your response? Will it be visceral or biblical?

Expiration Dates Exist?

That some gifts will cease or fade does not come as a shock to most believers. The Holy Spirit has told us so through the pen of the Apostle Paul:

> Love never ends. *As for prophecies, they will pass away; as for tongues, they will cease; as for knowledge, it will pass away. For we know in part and we prophesy in part, but when the perfect comes, the partial will pass away.* When I was a child, I spoke like a child, I thought like a child, I reasoned like a child. When I became a man, I gave up childish ways. For now we see in a mirror dimly, but then *face to face.* Now I know in part; then I shall know fully, even as I have been fully known. (1 Corinthians 13:8–12)

Some prefer the clarity of a more literal, word for word translation for 1 Corinthians 13:8–12. Here is how the New American Standard Bible renders the passage.

> Love never fails; but *if there are gifts of prophecy, they will be done away; if there are tongues, they will cease; if there is knowledge, it will be done away. For we know in part and we*

prophesy in part; but when the perfect comes, the partial will be done away. When I was a child, I used to speak like a child, think like a child, reason like a child; when I became a man, I did away with childish things. For now we see in a mirror dimly, but then *face to face*; now I know in part, but then I will know fully just as I also have been fully known. (1 Corinthians 13:8–12 [NASB])

Regardless of your preferred translation, Paul writes that there will be a cessation or fade of certain miraculous gifts. Only the gift of God's love endures forever. There can be no question that the gifts of tongues, words of knowledge, and prophecy will fade or cease to be (both translations reveal as much). These gifts, as Paul and the early Church knew them, will (one day) become unnecessary—that's what the Holy Spirit says. The question, therefore, is not *if* but *when*.

Theories Abound.
There can be no questions about whether some gifts will fade or cease to be—at least the gifts in this list (1 Corinthians 13:8–12). These gifts' cessation, fade, or expiration is connected to "the perfect."

Many suggest that the idea of "the perfect" is the second coming of Christ or the Eternal State (life in heaven). Once this world has ended or all believers are in heaven for eternity, the casting of sin, suffering, death, and hell into the Lake of Fire will eliminate the need for any kind of miracles. Preachers will be out of business as they, alongside other believers, will sit at the feet of Christ and hear him.

Others suggest the miracles worked by prophets and apostles are for a different age. Others suggest the perfect has already come as the completed Scriptures because the Greek word for "the perfect" can also mean complete, mature, or finished.[12] There are also those who suggest that "the perfect" pertains to the maturity and establishment of the New Testament Church outside of Jerusalem. Others combine both theories, believing "the perfect" pertains to the close of the canon of Scripture and establishing the Christian church internationally.

Which Theory is True?
When Christ conquers Satan and establishes the New Heaven and New Earth, spiritual gifts, even the miraculous (sign) gifts, will become obsolete. This view is supported by both cessationists and non-cessationists. In the eternal state, spiritual gifts—whether healing, prophecy, or any other sign gift—are no longer required.

Those who see "the perfect" as the close of the canon, like those who see the perfect as the maturity of the Church, view the sign gifts as temporary and, therefore, having faded or ceased. Those who combine these interpretations also tend toward the cessationist interpretation. All three point to the childhood-to-maturity analogy to support their definition and interpretation of "the perfect."

Those who support the interpretation that the perfect is the close of the canon of Scripture suggest the reference to "the partial" passing away suggests that with the sixty-six books of the completed Scriptures (in particular the book of Revelation), we have the whole picture of God's redemptive plan before us and see things as they are and will be. They propose that we no longer require prophets, dreams, seers, and the like because we have already a revelation made more sure. No new Scriptures

12   Walter Bauer, "τέλειος," *A Greek-English Lexicon of the New Testament and Other Early Christian Literature*, ed. Frederick William Danker, trans. William Arndt and F. Wilbur Gingrich, 3rd ed. (Chicago: University of Chicago Press, 2000), 995–96; Henry George Liddell, Robert Scott, Henry Stuart Jones, and Roderick McKenzie, "τέλειος," *A Greek-English Lexicon*, 9th rev. ed. (Oxford: Clarendon Press, 1996), 1769–70.

are being written. Therefore, miracles are no longer required to authenticate the message or the messenger because we have the revelation made more sure in writing, once and for all, handed down to the saints in the sixty-six books of the Bible.

A CASE FOR CESSATION

How is it that some argue against the ongoing existence of so-called miraculous gifts of the Holy Spirit? Those who would classify themselves as cessationists or non-continuationists argue along these fronts.

Lack of Evidence.

They declare that what passes today for speaking in tongues is often nothing more than gibberish. Some find their characterization offensive. But cessationists find what they perceive as disorder in so-called charismatic churches offensive, saying that more often than not, ecstatic utterances and the declaring of prophecies or words from God occur in violation of the Holy Spirit's specifications in 1 Corinthians 12 and 14. They also allege that much of speaking in tongues is not done decently and in order out of love for God based upon what 1 Corinthians 13:1–7 criticizes:

> If I speak in the tongues of men and of angels, but have not love, *I am a noisy gong or a clanging cymbal.* And if I have prophetic powers, and understand all mysteries and all knowledge, and if I have all faith, so as to remove mountains, *but have not love, I am nothing.* If I give away all I have, and if I deliver up my body to be burned, *but have not love, I gain nothing.* Love is patient and kind; love does not envy or boast; it is not arrogant or rude. It does not insist on its own way; it is not irritable or resentful; it does not rejoice at wrongdoing, but rejoices with the truth. Love bears all things, believes all things, hopes all things, endures all things.

These cessationists point to the Greek grammar of 1 Corinthians 13 noting the "ifs" and the grammatical mood (the subjunctive) to infer that such gifts were limited to the Apostles.[13] Many of those who believe in the cessation of such gifts suggest that the evidence in favor of continuation is often second-hand, subjective, spurious, or unreliable.

Hospitals and COVID-19.

The arguments against the continuation of the miraculous gifts of the Holy Spirit are not new. Those who argue for the cessation of the gifts query non-cessationists as to why healers do not engage in powerful evangelism by entering hospitals and healing the sick to glorify Christ. As I write during a worldwide pandemic, many who contend for the cessation of the miraculous gifts of the Holy Spirit ask why no one is going from place to place, healing the sick or raising the dead for the glory of God and the sake of others. Those who argue in favor of the continuation of the miraculous gifts of the Holy Spirit find these questions and this line of argumentation offensive. They often remind others of the words of Jesus that a crooked and evil generation seeks for a sign (Matthew 12:39). Cessationists, on the other hand, retort that all the signs and wonders seemingly performed in a worship service appear to them they are the wicked and perverse generation seeking signs and wonders. You can see how this quickly devolves into a heated debate rather than remaining a reasonable and biblical discussion among believers.

Biblical Evidence.

Those who believe in the cessation and fade of the miraculous gifts point to the Bible to make their case. This surprises many. The Bible does not provide an exact date beyond "when the perfect comes" for the cessation and fade of these miraculous gifts. However, cessationists

---

13   The scope of this study does not include the investigation of Greek grammar and syntax nor any in-depth exploration of lexical meanings or semantic ranges or domains.

argue the Bible documents the cessation and fade of these gifts in real time as one reads through the New Testament. They point out that in the Epistles of John, the Epistle of James, and the Epistles of Peter, there is no mention of anyone, let alone the authors, healing anyone. They argue that all references to such miracles refer to them in the past tense. They also point to the ministry of the Apostle Paul as their evidence for cessation.

Paul Performed Miracles.

From the Scriptures, it is impossible to argue that Paul did not perform miracles. I have already discussed some of them in the previous paragraphs and pages. Paul spoke in tongues. Paul cast out demons. Paul healed the sick. Paul raised the dead. A casual reading of the Book of Acts documents these facts. No one can argue otherwise.

Paul's Loss of Ability.

Those who believe the miraculous gifts of the Holy Spirit have ceased remind us that Paul, himself, foretold of this cessation or fade in 1 Corinthians 13:1–7. As evidence in favor of their position, they argue that the ministry of the Apostle Paul documents a cessation and fade in Paul. For example, they point to a gradual reduction in the frequency of healing. Early in Paul's ministry, Paul performed various signs and wonders. Later in Paul's ministry, he did not (or could not).

Paul's Illness.

Paul's letter to the Galatians points to an illness that Paul suffered from that was in some sense debilitating and, in some sense, disgusting.

> Brothers, I entreat you, become as I am, for I also have become as you are. You did me no wrong. *You know it was because of a bodily ailment that I preached the gospel to you at first, and though my condition was a trial to you, you did not*

> *scorn or despise me, but received me as an angel of God, as*
> *Christ Jesus.* What then has become of your blessedness? For
> I testify to you that, if possible, you would have gouged out
> your eyes and given them to me. Have I then become your
> enemy by telling you the truth? (Galatians 4:12–16)

The Apostle Paul describes his bodily ailment as "a trial" to those he preached to. It would seem his "condition" plagued him and those around him. Yet he did not heal himself. This missionary visit to Galatia was around 47 to 48 AD. Some wonder why Paul did not heal himself, having healed so many others.

In 2 Corinthians 12:7–10, the Apostle Paul describes his "thorn in the flesh." He could not remove it. Three times, Paul asked God to remove it. God refused as an object lesson. Paul penned this Epistle around 55 AD.

Illnesses of Paul's Associates.
Paul healed the sick and the injured, raising Eutychus from the dead after Eutychus' fall in the Book of Acts. However, Paul seems unable (unwilling?) to heal Epaphroditus, his close associate. Writing to the church at Philippi, Paul recounts his near loss of the beloved Epaphroditus.

> I have thought it necessary to send to you Epaphroditus my
> brother and fellow worker and fellow soldier, and your mes-
> senger and minister to my need, for he has been longing for
> you all and has been distressed *because you heard that he was*
> *ill. Indeed he was ill, near to death. But God had mercy on him,*
> *and not only on him but on me also, lest I should have sorrow*
> *upon sorrow.* I am the more eager to send him, therefore, that
> you may rejoice at seeing him again, *and that I may be less*
> *anxious.* (Philippians 2:25–28)

The Holy Spirit, speaking through the pen of the Apostle Paul, tells the church at Philippi that Epaphroditus became ill, and the illness progressed until he was near death. We read Paul was grieved and distressed by this. But God "showed mercy" and Epaphroditus recovered. Paul's comment is, *"God had mercy on him, and not only on him but on me also, lest I should have sorrow upon sorrow."* Why did not Paul heal this man? Paul loved him and was both grieved and worried. Why didn't (couldn't) Paul heal Epaphroditus? It was not from lack of concern or desire. Paul remarks that he will be less anxious by sending Epaphroditus to Philippi to, perhaps, further his recovery. Did Paul lack the ability to heal Epaphroditus? Had the gift ceased or faded? Cessationists argue that Paul no longer possessed the ability to heal by the time of the writing of Philippians, around 60 AD.

Cessationists offer two other examples of Paul's apparent inability, or loss of ability, to heal the sick, found in the Pastoral Epistles 1–2 Timothy. Some call them "passing comments" that reveal the inability to heal. In 1 Timothy 5:23, Paul encourages Timothy to drink water no longer only but mix it with wine because of his "frequent ailments." This comment results in two questions. First, as a spirit-filled believer, why didn't Timothy heal himself? Second, why didn't Paul heal Timothy (long distance) the way Jesus healed the royal official's son (John 4:43–54) or the Centurion's servant (Luke 7:1–10)? 1 Timothy was written around 62–63 AD.

Finally, there are Paul's comments in 2 Timothy 4:20. Here, writing to Timothy, Paul states, "Erastus remained at Corinth, and I left Trophimus, who was ill, at Miletus." Wouldn't Paul want to heal Trophimus instead of abandoning Trophimus at the town of Miletus? If Trophimus was so ill that he could not travel, why didn't Paul heal Trophimus? Those who do not believe the gifts continued beyond the ministry of the first Apostles point to incidents like this to argue for the cessation and fade of the miraculous gifts of the Holy Spirit. 2 Timothy was written around 64 AD.

Paul and "The Perfect."

These events in the life and ministry of Paul, coupled with his comments in 1 Corinthians 13:8–12, some point to the possibility that the so-called miraculous gifts are not for today. They point to the maturation and completion imagery in verses 10–12 to argue that the perfect is either the growth and maturation of the early church or the completion of what was then the partial canon of Scripture.

> Love never fails; but if there are gifts of prophecy, they will be done away; if there are tongues, they will cease; if there is knowledge, it will be done away. For we know in part and we prophesy in part; *but when the perfect comes, the partial will be done away. When I was a child, I used to speak like a child, think like a child, reason like a child; when I became a man, I did away with childish things. For now we see in a mirror dimly, but then face to face; now I know in part, but then I will know fully just as I also have been fully known.* (1 Corinthians 13:8–12 [NASB])

Some argue that Paul's apparent loss of ability points to the perfect in the form of either the maturation of the infant Church or the closing of the canon of Scripture (or both). They point to a gradual doing away with the sign gifts. Others offer the rebuttal that this is all circumstantial evidence. The counter rebuttal comes down to a somewhat blunt or crass demand to "show me" or "prove it." If miracles are an everyday occurrence, their existence should be easy to prove.

OPPORTUNITIES TO GLORIFY GOD

Some observe after the long Iraqi and Afghan Wars; there are so many broken and injured bodies and minds of war veterans that if the gift of healing were still operative, then healers could glorify God and do powerful evangelism by healing brain injuries, restoring limbs (as Jesus did), or raising the dead but they do not do so.

Those who contend that these miraculous gifts are for today point to testimonials and healing services on YouTube or one's television. Their "opponents" suggest that these videos are unsubstantiated. One wonders why some famous healer doesn't manifest God's infinite healing power by ever healing an individual with Down's Syndrome. Individuals with Down's Syndrome tend not to be skeptical and can have a great deal of trust and belief. One such act could silence all critics by healing the mind and body of such a person. Tens of thousands, hundreds of thousands, or millions could be convinced of God in Christ and be saved.

It is evident that miracles are not easily missed, which raises questions about the lack of substantial evidence, contact information, etc., readily accessible on platforms like YouTube, Zoom Meetings, smartphone camera footage, etc., showcasing the extraordinary powers of the Holy Spirit in action. It would be hard to miss a repeat of the parting of the Red Sea, raising a Lazarus-type from the dead, or walking on the water. Regardless of such questions, this issue will not be settled to anyone's satisfaction on this side of heaven. Win, lose, or draw, we do well to remember that spiritual gifts are a small, a lesser, part of the mission and ministry of the Holy Spirit.

CONCLUSION

No serious Christian I know of disputes the fact that ours is a supernatural and miracle-working God. God can work miracles today. Every person who is born again is a miracle of God's grace. Perhaps the larger question is whether the working of miracles is normative. The word miracle points to the rare nature of an event and the peculiar nature of the act. A miracle, such as healing or speaking in tongues, would be clearly noticeable and exceptionally uncommon, as it goes against the laws of nature. They represent divine intervention. Reading from Genesis to Revelation, we find miracles were rare. Most of the writing prophets did not work miracles. Yet the world seeks a sign. A wicked and evil generation seeks a sign. We do well to remember the teachings of Christ regarding the mission and ministry of the Holy Spirit, taking our cues from Jesus rather than the raucous and unruly church at Corinth. May neither we nor our gifts ever become distractions.

APPLICATION

Congratulations, you have just finished, or survived, a small survey of one of the more controversial chapters of this book. I hope it was beneficial. The question is, "What now."

Prayerfully Reflect.
Take time to pray, reflect, and ask yourself, "What have I learned, and what will I do with it?" Everything we learn about God from his word is for our encouragement and instruction that we might have hope (Romans 15:4). Regardless of your position on the continuation or non-continuation of the miraculous gifts of the Holy Spirit, you must be a good Berean and search the Scriptures to see what is true and what is not.

Ask If Change is Required.
Review all we have studied beyond the more controversial issues and questions about the gifts of the Holy Spirit. Was there anything you saw or read that changed how you thought of God, the Holy Spirit, God, the Son, and God, the Father? Did you learn something new? Can you give God thanks and glory for this?

Check Yourself.
What challenged you and why? Often, we hold beliefs and traditions that are purely experiential and biblically unsupportable. Looking to the word of God, the God-breathed sword of the Spirit, how will you respond? Will you make changes where changes are required?

FOR FURTHER THOUGHT

1. Review the lists of spiritual gifts (see above) and where they are found. How would you classify and explain them to someone new to the discussion?

2. Review the discussion of the greater gifts (i.e., teaching and preaching gifts) and the lesser gifts. What is the Holy Spirit telling us through the pen of the Apostle Paul? Can you relate this to 1 Corinthians 14:19?

3. Debate coaches tell us that the key to "defeating" an opponent's argument is stating his case in his own words to his satisfaction. Then, you have understood his point of view and can "attack it" (if necessary). Can you make a case for the cessation and fade of gifts employing the latter ministry of the Apostle Paul and 1 Corinthians 13:1–7?

4. Many suggest that so few miracles are seen today because our society (and too many Christians) are too skeptical. Read Matthew 17:20 and, taking into account that Jesus performed many miracles despite his critic's unbelief, explain why such an idea cannot be true. Tie your explanation into the fact that God worked many miracles through Moses despite the Israelites' lack of faith.

5. Given the relative unimportance of spiritual gifts to the mission and ministry of the Holy Spirit, do some seem to emphasize them at great cost to the work of the Kingdom? What changes should they make?

6. Are the sign (the miraculous) gifts of the Holy Spirit the greater gifts? What does the Bible show in 1 Corinthians 12:28–31? Which are more important, the greater or lesser gifts? Can you relate this to 1 Corinthians 13:1–17? Looking back at question three, could you restate the argument of one who disagrees with you to their satisfaction?

8

IN CONCLUSION:

The end of the matter; all has been heard.
Fear God and keep his commandments, for this is
the whole duty of man. (Ecclesiastes 12:13)

TAKEAWAYS

I hope you have found this initial foray into this important topic helpful or thought-provoking. Know that we have only scratched the surface when it comes to the Holy Spirit. We've not discussed the Holy Spirit in the Old Testament or what is involved in his indwelling us. We've not broached topics like "Can a Christian, indwelt by the Holy Spirit, suffer demonic possession?" There is so much more territory to cover and discuss.

What Have You Learned?
Most people only know of the Holy Spirit what they hear on the radio or watch on a screen. I hope you've learned most of what we need to know about the Holy Spirit from Jesus in John's Gospel.

Maybe a cultist like a Jehovah's Witness will knock on your door someday. Perhaps you've learned a manageable number of verses to challenge her and assure yourself that the Holy Spirit is God and the Trinity exists.

Maybe you've learned enough to make a modalist who denies the Trinity stop and think and search the Scriptures for themselves. By now, you should know that the Holy Spirit is not a Force, a "she," or an "it" but a "he." Jesus says so!

If anything, I hope you have learned that too many people sin against God by a cavalier and disorderly pattern of behavior in churches around the world by unrestrained behavior forbidden by the Spirit, Himself, in 1 Corinthians 14:27–33. We hope you've learned to behave in church and what churches and church leaderships to avoid—those who defy the Holy Spirit by prophesying in droves or "speaking in tongues" several at a time, all at once in defiance of the Holy Spirit.

Where the Bible Fits In.
You may recall that we observed that the best way to understand an individual comes through what he or she has to say about himself or herself. Often, Christians look to "Rock Star" pastors and larger-than-life personalities (and even athletes) to learn about the Holy Spirit. The Holy Spirit has written extensively about himself in the God-breathed Scriptures. He has much to say to you if you only pick up and read.

You may have noticed I have an annoying habit (to some) of writing things like "the Holy Spirit writes through the pen of the Apostle..." There's a reason for that. Too often, people look to some experience, celebrity teacher, or other person of influence to give them "a word" from or on the Holy Spirit. Sometimes, these "revelations" contradict Scripture. That should tell you something because the Holy Spirit does not lie, nor does he contradict Himself (Numbers 23:19). Look to the book! Look *at* the book! God's word has something to say about every inch of thread that makes up the fabric of our existence. Pick up and read!

What's Next?

Regardless of your position and previous tradition, take a step back and ask, "What does the Bible have to say about my beliefs and what I've experienced?" Will you elevate experience over Scripture? Will you weigh and evaluate your experiences in the scales of Scripture as you view your world and your experiences through the lens of Scripture?

As for you, I hope there are years and years of rich ministry ahead as you do what you do for the glory of God, the good of others, and your spiritual growth. God has raised you up for such a time as this to be a part of his kingdom work where Christians change this world one soul at a time with the message of Jesus Christ. Remember the promise of Jesus to his disciples in the last hours before his arrest because it is a promise to you and me.

> If you love me, you will keep my commandments. And I will ask the Father, and he will give you another Helper, to be with you forever, even the Spirit of truth, whom the world cannot receive, because it neither sees him nor knows him. You know him; he dwells with you and will be in you. (John 14:15–17)

Grace to you.